Philip Roth

PATRIMONY

Philip Roth received the 1960 National Book Award
in Fiction for *Goodbye, Columbus*. In the last decade
he has twice received the National Book Critics
Circle Award—in 1987 for the novel *The Counterlife*
and in 1992 for *Patrimony*. His other books include
the trilogy and epilogue *Zuckerman Bound*; the novels *Letting Go*, *My Life as a Man*, and *The Professor
of Desire*; the political satire *Our Gang*; and the
autobiography *The Facts*. *Operation Shylock* won the
PEN/Faulkner Award for Fiction and was chosen by
Time magazine as the best American novel of 1993.
His latest book is *Sabbath's Theater*, which received
the 1995 National Book Award for Fiction.

INTERNATIONAL

Books by Philip Roth

Sabbath's Theater
Operation Shylock
Patrimony
Deception
The Facts
The Counterlife
Zuckerman Bound
The Prague Orgy
The Anatomy Lesson
Zuckerman Unbound
The Ghost Writer
The Professor of Desire
Reading Myself and Others
My Life as a Man
The Great American Novel
The Breast
Our Gang
Portnoy's Complaint
When She Was Good
Letting Go
Goodbye, Columbus

PATRIMONY

Philip Roth

PATRIMONY

A True Story

VINTAGE INTERNATIONAL

Vintage Books

A Division of Random House, Inc.

New York

FIRST VINTAGE INTERNATIONAL EDITION, APRIL 1996

Copyright © 1991 by Philip Roth

All rights reserved under International and Pan-American Copyright Conven-
tions. Published in the United States by Vintage Books, a division of Random
House, Inc., New York, and simultaneously in Canada by
Random House of Canada Limited, Toronto. Originally published in the
United States in hardcover by Simon & Schuster Inc.,
New York, in 1991.

Library of Congress Cataloging-in-Publication Data
Roth, Philip.
Patrimony / by Philip Roth. — 1st Vintage International ed.
p. cm.
ISBN 0-679-75293-5
1. Roth, Philip—Family. 2. Novelists, American—20th century—Family
relationships. 3. Fathers and sons—United States—Biography.
4. Roth family. I. Title.
[PS3568.0855Z468 1996]
813'.54—dc20
[B] 95-43453
CIP

Random House Web address: http://www.randomhouse.com/

Frontispiece photograph: Herman, 36, Sandy, 9, and Philip Roth, 4;
Bradley Beach, New Jersey, August 1937.

Printed in the United States of America
10 9 8 7 6 5 4 3 2 1

For our family,
the living and the dead

PATRIMONY

1

Well, What Do You Think?

My father had lost most of the sight in his right eye by the time he'd reached eighty-six, but otherwise he seemed in phenomenal health for a man his age when he came down with what the Florida doctor diagnosed, incorrectly, as Bell's palsy, a viral infection that causes paralysis, usually temporary, to one side of the face.

The paralysis appeared, out of nowhere, the day after he had flown from New Jersey to West Palm Beach to spend the winter months sharing a sublet apartment with a retired bookkeeper of seventy, Lillian Beloff, who lived upstairs from him in Elizabeth and with whom he had become romantically involved a year after my mother died in 1981. At the West Palm airport, he had been feeling so fit that he hadn't even bothered with a porter (whom, besides, he would have had to tip) and carried his own luggage from the baggage area all the way out to the taxi stand. Then the next morning, in the bathroom mirror, he saw that half his face was no longer his. What had looked like him the day before now looked like nobody—the lower lid of the bad eye bagged downward, revealing the lid's inner lining, the cheek on that side had gone slack and lifeless as though beneath the bone had been filleted, and his lips were no longer straight but drawn down diagonally across his face.

With his hand he pushed the right cheek back to where it had been the night before, holding it there for the count of ten. He did this repeatedly that morning—and every day thereafter—but when he let go, it wouldn't stay. He tried to tell himself that he had lain the wrong way in bed, that his skin was simply furrowed from sleep, but what he believed was that he'd had a stroke. His father had been crippled by a stroke back in the early 1940s, and once he'd become an old man himself, he said to me several times, "I don't want to go the way he did. I don't want to lie there like that. That's my worst fear." He told me how he used to stop off to see his father at the hospital early in the morning on the way downtown to the office and again on his way home at night. Twice a day he lit cigarettes and stuck them in his father's mouth for him and in the evening he sat beside the bed and read to him from the Yiddish paper. Immobilized and helpless, with only his cigarettes to soothe him, Sender Roth lingered for almost a year, and until a second stroke finished him off late one night in 1942, my father, twice each day, sat and watched him die.

The doctor who told my father that he had Bell's palsy assured him that in a short time most, if not all, of the facial paralysis would be gone. And within days of his getting this prognosis, it was confirmed for him by three different people, in just his section of the vast condominium development, who'd had the same ailment and recovered. One of them had had to wait for nearly four months, but eventually the paralysis went away as mysteriously as it had come.

His didn't go away.

He soon couldn't hear out of his right ear. The Florida doctor examined the ear and measured the hearing loss, but told him it had nothing to do with the Bell's palsy. It was just something that happened with age—he had probably been losing the hearing in the right ear as gradually as he had lost the sight in the right eye and only now had noticed it. This

time when my father asked how much longer the
doctor thought he'd have to wait before the Bell's
palsy disappeared, the doctor told him that in cases
that continued as long as his had, it sometimes never
disappeared. Look, count your blessings, the doctor
said; except for a blind eye, a deaf ear, and a half-
paralyzed face, he was as healthy as a man twenty
years younger.

When I phoned each Sunday, I could hear that
as a consequence of the drooping mouth, his speech
had become slurred and difficult to follow—he
sounded at times like someone fresh from the dental
chair whose novocaine hadn't worn off; when I flew
to Florida to see him, I was startled to find him looking as though he might not be able to speak at all.

"Well," he said, in the lobby of my hotel, where
I was meeting Lil and him for dinner, "what do you
think?" Those were his first words, even as I bent
over to kiss him. He was sunk down beside Lil in a
tapestried love seat, but his face was aimed straight
up at me so that I could see what had happened.
Over the last year he had intermittently been wearing
a black patch over his blind eye to prevent the light
and the wind from irritating it, and what with the eye
patch, the cheek, the mouth, and the fact that he had
lost a lot of weight, he seemed to me gruesomely
transformed—in the five weeks since I'd last seen
him in Elizabeth—into an enfeebled old man. It was
hard to believe that only some six years earlier, the
winter after my mother's death, when he was sharing
the Bal Harbour apartment of his old friend Bill

Weber, he'd had no difficulty convincing the wealthy widows in the building—who'd immediately begun to swarm with interest around the gregarious new widower in the fresh seersucker jacket and pastel trousers—that he had only just reached seventy, even though we had all gathered together to mark his eightieth birthday the summer before in my house in Connecticut.

At dinner in the hotel I began to understand how much of a handicap the Bell's palsy was, in addition to being disfiguring. He could now drink successfully only by using a straw; otherwise the liquid ran out the paralyzed half of his mouth. And eating was a bite-by-bite effort, laden with frustration and embarrassment. Reluctantly he agreed, after spotting his tie with his soup, to allow Lil to wrap a napkin around his neck—there was already a napkin across his lap, more or less protecting his trousers. Occasionally Lil reached over with her own napkin and, to his disgruntlement, removed a piece of food that had slipped out of his mouth and adhered to his chin without his knowing it. Several times she reminded him to put less food on his fork and to try, with each bite, to take into his mouth a little less than he was accustomed to. "Yeah," he mumbled, staring disconsolately into his plate, "yeah, sure," and after two or three bites he forgot. It was because eating had become a depressing ordeal that he had lost all this weight and looked so pathetically undernourished.

What made everything still more difficult was

that cataracts in both his eyes had thickened in recent months, so that even the sight in his one good
eye had grown blurry. For several years my ophthalmologist in New York, David Krohn, had been following the progress of my father's cataracts and
dealing with his deteriorating vision, and when, in
March, my father returned to New Jersey from his
unhappy stay in Florida, he went to New York to urge
David to remove the cataract from the good eye; because he was powerless to do anything about the
Bell's palsy, he was particularly eager that some ac-
tion be taken toward restoring his sight. But late in
the afternoon following my father's visit, David
phoned to say that he was reluctant to operate on the
eye until further tests had determined the cause of
the facial paralysis and the hearing loss. He wasn't
convinced that it was Bell's palsy.

He was right not to be. Harold Wasserman, my
father's New Jersey physician, had arranged locally
for the MRI scan that David ordered, and when Harold received the report from the lab, he called me
early that evening to give me the results. My father
had a brain tumor, "a massive tumor," Harold called
it, and though with MRI pictures one couldn't distin-
guish between a benign and a malignant tumor, Harold said, "Either way, those tumors kill you." The
next step was to consult with a neurosurgeon, to determine precisely the kind of tumor it was and what,
if anything, might be done. "I'm not optimistic,"
Harold said, "and neither should you be."

I managed to get my father to the neurosurgeon without telling him what the MRI had already disclosed. I lied and said that the tests showed nothing, but that David, being extra cautious, wanted to get one last opinion on the facial paralysis before he went ahead with the cataract removal. In the meantime, I arranged for the MRI pictures to be sent to the Essex House Hotel in New York. Claire Bloom and I were temporarily living there while we were looking for an apartment—we were planning to find a place in Manhattan after ten years of dividing our lives between her house in London and mine in Connecticut.

In fact, only about a week before the MRI pictures of my father's brain, along with the radiologist's report, were delivered to the hotel in an oversized envelope, Claire had returned to London to see her daughter and to look after repairs on her house and to meet with her accountant over a long-standing negotiation with the British tax authorities. She had been yearning terribly for London, and the month's visit was designed not merely to let her attend to practical matters but to take the edge off her homesickness. I suppose that if my father's tumor had been discovered earlier, when Claire was with me, my preoccupation with him would not have been so all-consuming, and—at least in the evenings—I might have been less likely to become as depressed about his illness as I did on my own. Yet even at the time it seemed to me that Claire's absence—along with the fact that in a hotel, feeling transient and homeless, I was finding it impossible to write—was a peculiarly opportune fortuity: with no other responsibilities, I could attend entirely to him.

Being by myself also allowed me to be as emotional as I felt, without having to put up a manly or mature or philosophical front. Alone, when I felt like crying I cried, and I never felt more like it than when I removed from the envelope the series of pictures of his brain—and not because I could readily identify the tumor invading the brain but simply because it *was* his brain, my father's brain, what prompted him to think the blunt way he thought, speak the emphatic way he spoke, reason the emotional way he reasoned, decide the impulsive way he decided. This was the tissue that had manufactured his set of endless worries and sustained for more than eight decades his stubborn self-discipline, the source of everything that had so frustrated me as his adolescent son, the thing that had ruled our fate back when he was all-powerful and determining our purpose, and now it was being compressed and displaced and destroyed because of "a large mass predominantly located within the region of the right cerebellopontine angles and prepontine cisterns. There is extension of the mass into the right cavernous sinus with encasement of the carotid artery . . ." I didn't know where to find the cerebellopontine angles or prepontine cisterns, but reading in the radiologist's report that the carotid artery was encased in the tumor was, for me, as good as reading his death sentence. "There is also apparent destruction of the right pe-

trous apex. There is significant posterior displace-
ment and compression of the pons and right cerebel-
lar peduncle by this mass . . ."

I was alone and without inhibition, and so, while
the pictures of his brain, photographed from every
angle, lay spread across the hotel bed, I made no
effort to fight back anything. Maybe the impact
wasn't quite what it would have been had I been
holding that brain in the palms of my hands, but it
was along those lines. God's will erupted out of a
burning bush and, no less miraculously, Herman
Roth's had issued forth all these years from this bul-
bous organ. I had seen my father's brain, and everything and nothing was revealed. A mystery scarcely
short of divine, the brain, even in the case of a retired
insurance man with an eighth-grade education from
Newark's Thirteenth Avenue School.

My nephew Seth drove my father up to Millburn to
see the neurosurgeon, Dr. Meyerson, in his suburban
office. I had arranged for my father to see him there
rather than at Newark's University Hospital because
I thought the mere location of the doctor's hospital
office, which I had been told was in the oncology
wing, would signal to him that he had a cancer, when
no such diagnosis had been made and he didn't even
know yet that he had the tumor. This way he
wouldn't be frightened out of his skin, at least for a
while.

And when I spoke to Dr. Meyerson on the phone

later that day, he told me that a tumor like my father's, located in front of the brain stem, was benign about ninety-five percent of the time. According to Meyerson, the tumor could have been growing there for as long as ten years; but the recent onset of facial paralysis and deafness in the right ear suggested that "in a relatively short time," as he put it, "it'll get much worse." It was still possible, however, to remove it surgically. He told me that seventy-five percent of those operated on survive and are better, ten percent die on the table, and another fifteen percent either die shortly afterward or are left worse.

"If he survives," I asked, "what is the convalescence like?"

"It's difficult. He'd be in a convalescent home for a month—maybe as long as two or three months."

"It's hell, in other words."

"It's rough," he said, "but do nothing and it could be rougher."

I wasn't about to give Meyerson's news to my father on the phone, and so the next morning, when I called at around nine, I said I was going to come over to Elizabeth to see him.

"So, it's that bad," he said.

"Let me drive over and we'll sit down and talk about it."

"Do I have cancer?" he asked me.

"No, you don't have cancer."

"What is it then?"

"Be patient for another hour and I'll be there and tell you exactly what the situation is."

"I want to know now."

"I'll only be an hour—less than an hour," I said, convinced that it was better for him to have to wait, however frightened he was, than to tell him flat out on the phone and have him sitting alone, in shock, until I arrived.

It was probably no wonder, given the task I was about to perform, that when I got off the turnpike in Elizabeth, I missed the fork in the exit road that would have taken me into North Avenue and directly to my father's apartment building a few blocks away. Instead, I wound up on a stretch of New Jersey highway that, a mile or two on, passed right alongside the cemetery where my mother had been buried seven years before. I didn't believe there was anything mystical about how I'd got there, but it was amazing nonetheless to see where the twenty-minute drive from Manhattan had landed me.

I had been to the cemetery only twice, first on the day of her funeral in 1981 and the following year, when I took my father out to see her stone. Both times we had driven from Elizabeth proper and not from Manhattan, and so I hadn't known that the cemetery could even be reached by the turnpike. And had I actually been driving over to find the cemetery that day, I more than likely would have lost my way in the complex of turnoffs to Newark Airport, Port Newark, Port Elizabeth, and back to downtown

Newark. Though I wasn't searching for that cemetery either consciously or unconsciously, on the
morning when I was to tell my father of the brain
tumor that would kill him, I had flawlessly traveled
the straightest possible route from my Manhattan
hotel to my mother's grave and the grave site beside
hers where he was to be buried.

I hadn't wanted to leave my father waiting any
longer than was absolutely necessary, yet having arrived where I had, I was unable to continue on by as
though nothing unusual had happened. I didn't expect to learn anything new by going off and standing
at the foot of my mother's grave that morning; I
didn't expect to be comforted or strengthened by her
memory or better prepared somehow to help my father through his affliction; nor did I figure I'd be
weakened substantially seeing his plot beside hers.
The accident of a wrong turn had brought me there,
and all I did by getting out of the car and entering
the cemetery to find her grave was to bow to its impelling force. My mother and the other dead had
been brought here by the impelling force of what
was, after all, a more unlikely accident—having once
lived.

I find that while visiting a grave one has thoughts
that are more or less anybody's thoughts and, leaving
aside the matter of eloquence, don't differ much
from Hamlet's contemplating the skull of Yorick.
There seems little to be thought or said that isn't a
variant of "he hath borne me on his back a thousand

times." At a cemetery you are generally reminded of just how narrow and banal your thinking is on this subject. Oh, you can try talking to the dead if you feel that'll help; you can begin, as I did that morning, by saying, "Well, Ma . . ." but it's hard not to know —if you even get beyond a first sentence—that you might as well be conversing with the column of vertebrae hanging in the osteopath's office. You can make them promises, catch them up on the news, ask for their understanding, their forgiveness, for their love—or you can take the other, the active approach, you can pull weeds, tidy the gravel, finger the letters carved in the tombstone; you can even get down and place your hands directly above their remains—touching the ground, *their* ground, you can shut your eyes and remember what they were like when they were still with you. But nothing is altered by these recollections, except that the dead seem even more distant and out of reach than they did when you were driving in the car ten minutes earlier. If there's no one in the cemetery to observe you, you can do some pretty crazy things to make the dead seem something other than dead. But even if you succeed and get yourself worked up enough *to feel their presence*, you still walk away without them. What cemeteries prove, at least to people like me, is not that the dead are present but that they are gone. They are gone and, as yet, we aren't. This is fundamental and, however unacceptable, grasped easily enough.

2

Mommy, Mommy,
Where Are You, Mommy?

My father's retirement pension from Metropolitan Life provided him with more than enough to live on in the modest no-frills style that seemed to him natural and sufficient for someone who grew up in near-poverty, worked slavishly for some forty years to give his family a secure, if simple, home life, and lacked the slightest interest in conspicuous con-

sumption, ostentation, or luxury. In addition to the
pension he'd been receiving now for twenty-three
years, he drew Social Security income and the interest on his accumulated wealth—some eighty thousand dollars' worth of savings accounts, CDs, and
municipal bonds. Despite his solid financial situation, however, in advanced old age he had become
annoyingly tight about spending anything on himself.
Though he did not hesitate to give generous gifts to
his two grandsons whenever they needed money, he
was continually saving inconsequential sums that de-
prived him of things he himself liked or needed.

Among the more distressing economies was his
refusal to buy his own *New York Times*. He worshiped
that paper and loved to spend the morning reading it
through, but now, instead of buying his own, he
waited all day long to have a copy passed on to him
by somebody in his building who had been feckless
enough to fork over the thirty-five cents for it. He'd
also given up buying the *Star-Ledger*, a fifteen-cent
daily that, along with the defunct *Newark News*, he
had read ever since I was a child and it was called
the *Newark Star-Eagle*. He also refused to retain, on
a weekly basis, the cleaning woman who used to help
my mother with the apartment and the laundry. The
woman now came one day a month, and he cleaned
the apartment himself the rest of the time. "What
else do I have to do?" he asked. But as he was nearly
blind in one eye and had a cataract thickening in the
other and was no longer as agile as he liked to imag-

ine, no matter how hard he worked the job he did do was awful. The bathroom smelled, the carpets were dirty, and few of the appliances in the kitchen could have passed muster with a health inspector who hadn't been bribed.

It was a comfortably furnished, rather ordinary three-room apartment, decorated with neither flair nor bad taste. The living room carpet was a pleasant avocado green and the furniture there mostly antique reproductions, and on the walls were two large reproductions (chosen for my parents nearly forty years back by my brother, who had been to art school) of Gauguin landscapes framed in wormwood as well as an expressionistic portrait that my brother had painted of my father in his early seventies. There were thriving plants by the row of windows that faced a quiet, tree-lined, residential street to the south; there were photos in every room—of children, grandchildren, daughters-in-law, nephews, nieces— and the few books on the shelves in the dining area were either by me or on Jewish subjects. Aside from the lamps, which were a little glitzily ornate and sur- prisingly uncharacteristic of my mother's prim, everything-in-its-place aesthetic, it was a warm, wel- coming apartment whose gleaming appearance—at least when my mother was still alive—was somewhat in contrast to the depressing lobby and hallways of the thirty-year-old building, which were uninvitingly bare and growing slightly dilapidated.

Ever since my father had been alone, when I

was visiting, I'd sometimes wind up, after having used the toilet, scouring the sink, cleaning the soap dish, and rinsing out the toothbrush glass before I returned to sit with him in the living room. He insisted on washing his underclothes and his socks in the bathroom rather than parting with the few quarters that it cost to use the washer/dryer in the basement laundry room; every time I came to see him, there were his grayish, misshapen things draped over wire hangers on the shower rod and the towel racks. Though he prided himself on being nattily dressed and always enjoyed putting on a nicely tailored new sports jacket or a three-piece Hickey-Freeman suit (enjoyed it particularly when he'd bought it at an end-of-season sale), he had taken to cutting corners on whatever wasn't visible to anyone else. His pajamas and handkerchiefs, like his underwear and socks, looked as though they hadn't been replaced since my mother's death.

When I got to his apartment that morning—after the inadvertent visit to my mother's grave—I quickly excused myself and went off to the toilet. First I'd missed a turnoff, and now in the bathroom I was taking another few minutes to rehearse for a final time the best way to tell him about the tumor. While I stood over the bowl, his undergarments hung all around me like remnants strung out by a farmer to scare the birds away. On the open shelves above the toilet, where there was an assortment of prescription drugs, as well as his Polident, Vaseline, and Ascriptin, his boxes of tissues, Q-tips, and absorbent cotton, I spotted the shaving mug that had once been my grandfather's; in it my father kept his razor and a tube of shaving cream. The mug was pale blue porcelain; a delicate floral design enclosed a wide white panel at the front, and inside the panel the name "S. Roth" and the date "1912" were inscribed in faded gold Gothic lettering. The mug was our one family heirloom as far as I knew, aside from a handful of antique snapshots the only thing tangible that anyone had cared to save from the immigrant years in Newark. I had been intrigued by it ever since my grandfather had died a month short of my seventh birthday and it made its way into our Newark bathroom, back when my father was still shaving with a bristle brush and shaving soap.

Sender Roth had been a remote, mysterious presence to me as a small boy, an elongated man with an undersized head—the forebear whom my own skeleton most resembles—and about whom all I knew was that he smoked all day long, spoke only Yiddish, and wasn't much given to fondling the American grandchildren when we all showed up with our parents on Sundays. After his death, the shaving mug in our bathroom brought him much more fully to life for me, not as a grandfather but, even more interestingly then, as an ordinary man among men, a customer of a barbershop where his mug was kept on a shelf with the mugs of the other neighborhood immigrants. It reassured me as a child to think that

in that household where, according to all reports,
there was never a penny to spare, a dime was set
aside every week for him to go to the barbershop and
get his Sabbath shave.

My grandfather Roth had studied to be a rabbi
in Polish Galicia, in a small town not far from Lem-
berg, but when he arrived in America alone in 1897,
without his wife and his three sons (my uncles Charlie, Morris, and Ed), he took a job in a hat factory to
earn the money to bring his family over and worked
there more or less most of his life. There were seven
children born between 1890 and 1914, six sons and a
daughter, and all but the last two of the boys and the
one girl left school after the eighth grade to find jobs
to help support the family. The shaving mug inscribed "S. Roth" had seemed to free my grandfather—if only momentarily, if only for those few
minutes he quietly sat being shaved in the barber's
chair late on a Friday afternoon—from the dour exi-
gencies that had trapped him and that, I imagined,
accounted for his austere, uncommunicative nature.
His mug emitted the aura of an archaeological find,
an artifact signaling an unexpected level of cultural
refinement, an astonishing superfluity in an otherwise cramped and obstructed existence—in our ordinary little Newark bathroom, it had the impact on
me of a Greek vase depicting the mythic origins of
the race.

By 1988 what amazed me about it was that my
father hadn't thrown it out or given it away. Over the

years, when it was within his power, he had gotten
rid of just about everything "useless" to which any
of us might have been thought to have a sentimental
attachment. Though these seizures of largess were,
on the whole, admirably motivated, they sometimes
lacked sensitivity to innate property rights. So eager
was he to answer the need (real or imagined) of the
recipient that he did not always think about the effect
of his impulsiveness on the unwitting donor.

My two-volume stamp collection, for instance,
studiously acquired by me throughout my late grade
school years—a collection partially inspired by the
example of the country's most famous philatelist,
Franklin Delano Roosevelt, and underwritten with
virtually all my riches—he gave away to a great-
nephew of his the year I went off to college. I didn't
know this until ten years later, when I was thinking
of drawing on my scholarly discoveries as a boy
stamp collector for an episode in a piece of fiction
and went down to my parents' house in Moorestown
to get the albums out of the attic. It was only after I
had searched thoroughly, but in vain, through the
cartons I'd stored there that my mother reluctantly
—and not until we were off alone together—explained how they had come to disappear. She assured me that she had tried to stop him, that she had
told him that my stamps weren't his to dispose of,
but he wouldn't listen. He told her that I was grown
up, away at college, didn't "use" the stamps anymore, whereas Chickie, his great-nephew, could

bring them with him to school, et cetera, et cetera, et cetera. I suppose I could have found out if any part of my collection even existed any longer by contacting Chickie—a relative who was virtually a stranger to me and by then a young married man—but I decided to let the whole thing drop. I was terrifically irritated to hear what he had done—and, when I remembered how much of my childhood had gone into that collection, genuinely pained—but as it was so long ago that he had done it and as I had rather more difficult problems to deal with (I was in the midst of an acrimonious marital separation) I said nothing to him. And even if I had been inclined to, it would have been no easier for me to criticize him to his face at twenty-eight than it had been at eighteen or eight, since his most blatantly thoughtless acts were invariably ignited by this spontaneous impulse to support, to assist, to rescue, to save, prompted by the conviction that what he was doing—giving away my stamps, for example—was generous, helpful, and morally or educationally efficacious.

I believe another motive was operating in him— one harder to fathom and name—when we came back from burying my mother in May of 1981, and even as the apartment began filling up with family and friends, he disappeared into the bedroom and started emptying her bureau drawers and sorting through the clothes in her closet. I was still at the door with my brother, welcoming the mourners who'd followed us back from the cemetery, and so I

wouldn't right off have known what he was up to had
not my mother's sister Millie rushed out of the bedroom and down the hallway calling for help. "You
better go in there and do something, darling," she
whispered into my ear; "your father's throwing
everything out."

Not even my opening the bedroom door and
coming into the room and firmly saying, "Dad, what
are you doing?" did anything to slow him down. The
bed was already strewn with dresses, coats, skirts,
and blouses pulled from the closet, and he was now
busily chucking things from a corner of her lowest
bureau drawer into a plastic garbage bag. I put my
hand on his shoulder and gripped it forcefully. "People are here for you," I said; "they want to see you,
to talk to you—" "What good is this stuff anymore?
It's no good to me hanging here. This stuff can go to
Jewish relief—it's in mint condition—" "Stop,
please—just stop. There's time for all this later.
We'll do it together later. Stop throwing things out,"
I said. "Pull yourself together. Go into the living
room where you're needed."

But he *was* pulled together. He didn't appear to
be either in a daze or in the throes of a hysterical fit
—he was simply doing what he had done all his life:
the next difficult job. Thirty minutes before, we had
buried her body; now to dispose of her things.

I ushered him out of the bedroom, and once
among the guests who had come to offer condo-
lences, he immediately began talking away, assuring

everyone that he was fine. I returned to the bedroom
to remove from the garbage bag the pile of mementos
that he'd already discarded and that my mother had
neatly and carefully saved over the years—among
them, in a tiny brown envelope, my Phi Beta Kappa
key, which she had coveted, a collection of programs
to family graduation exercises, birthday cards from
my brother and me, a handful of telegrams announcing good news, clippings friends had sent her about
me and my books, specially prized snapshots of her
two grandsons as small boys. They were all items for
which my father could imagine no function now that
she who had treasured them was gone, the sentimental keepsakes of someone whose sentiments had
been snuffed out forever two nights earlier at a seafood restaurant where, as was their custom, they had
gone with friends for Sunday night dinner. My
mother had just been served clam chowder, a favorite dish of hers; to everyone's surprise she had announced, "I don't want this soup"; and those were
her last words—a moment later she was dead of a
massive coronary.

It was my father's primitivism that stunned me.
Standing all alone emptying her drawers and her
closets, he seemed driven by some instinct that
might be natural to a wild beast or an aboriginal
tribesman but ran counter to just about every mourn-
ing rite that had evolved in civilized societies to mitigate the sense of loss among those who survive the
death of a loved one. Yet there was also something

almost admirable in this pitilessly realistic determi-
nation to acknowledge, instantaneously, that he was
now an old man living alone and that symbolic relics
were no substitute for the real companion of fifty-five
years. It seemed to me that it was not out of fear of
her things and their ghostlike power that he wanted
to rid the apartment of them without delay—to bury
them now, too—but because he refused to sidestep
the most brutal of all facts.

Never in his life, as far as I knew, had he been
one to try to elude the force of a dreadful blow, and
yet, as I later learned, on the evening of her death
he had fled from her corpse. This occurred not
at the restaurant, where she had in fact died, but at
the hospital, where she was declared dead after the
paramedics had worked in vain to revive her on the
ambulance ride from the restaurant to the emergency
room. At the hospital, they pushed her stretcher into
a cubicle of its own, and when my father, who had
followed the ambulance in his car, went in by himself
to look at her, he could not stand to see what he saw
and so he ran. It was months before he could speak
about this to anyone; and when he did, it wasn't to
me or to my brother but to Claire, who, as a woman,
could grant him the womanly absolution he required
to begin to shed his shame.

Though he wasn't himself equipped to account
for why he'd run away like that, I wondered if it
hadn't something to do with his realizing that he
might have contributed to the heart attack by push-

ing my mother that afternoon to walk beyond her
endurance. She had been suffering for some time
from severe shortness of breath and, unknown to me,
from angina; during the previous winter there had
also been a long siege of arthritic pain that had de-
moralized her terribly. That winter she'd had all she
could do just to sit up comfortably in a chair, but on
the day she died, because the May weather was so
beautiful and she was finally out of doors getting
some exercise, they'd walked as far as the drugstore,
three very long city blocks away, and then, because
he insisted it would be good for her, they'd also
walked all the way home. According to Aunt Millie
—whom my mother had phoned before they went out
for the evening—by the time they'd reached the
drugstore, she was already hopelessly exhausted. "I
didn't think I could get back," she'd reported to my
aunt, but instead of calling a taxi or waiting for a bus,
they had rested a little on a nearby bench, and then
he'd got her up on her feet for the return trek. "You
know your father," my aunt had said to me. "He told
her she could do it." She had spent the rest of the
afternoon on the bed, trying to recover enough
strength to go out to dinner.

　　As it happened, only an hour or so before they'd
left for their walk, I'd made my customary Sunday
call from England and told her playfully that I expected her to go a mile with me down the country
road outside my house when she and my father came
to visit that summer. She replied, "I don't know if

it'll be a mile, dear, but I'll try." She was sounding bright and confident for the first time in months and could well have gone off that afternoon hoping to begin to prepare herself for our summer stroll.

In fact, when I arrived back in America the next day and took a taxi from Kennedy directly over to Elizabeth, my father's first words to me were "Well, she won't be taking that walk, Phil." He was in her reclining chair, his body decrepit, his face battered-looking and drained of all life. I thought (not incorrectly, as it turned out), "This is what he will look like when *he* is dead." My brother, Sandy, and his wife, Helen, had arrived earlier in the day from Chicago and were at the apartment when I got there. Sandy had already been to the funeral home to arrange for the burial the next day. Before he'd gone, my father had spoken on the phone to the elderly funeral director, a man with whom my mother had attended Elizabeth's Battin High around the end of the First World War. My father, in tears, had told him, "Take care of her body, take good care of it, Higgins," then for the rest of the day he went on weeping, there in that chair in which she would stretch out after supper and try to get some relief from her arthritis while they watched the news together. "She ordered New England clam chowder," he told me as I kneeled beside him, still in my coat and holding his hand, "and I ordered Manhattan. When it came she said, 'I don't want this soup.' I said, 'Take mine—we'll switch,' but she was gone.

Just slumped forward. Didn't even fall. Made no
trouble for anyone. The way she always did everything."

Over and over again he recounted for me the
pure prosaicness of the seconds preceding her ex-
tinction, while all the while I was thinking, "What
are we going to do with this old guy?" To have min-
istered to my mother's needs, had she been the elderly survivor of their marriage, would have seemed
manageable and natural enough; it was she who was
the repository of our family past, the historian of our
childhood and growing up, and, as I now realized, it
was she around whose quietly efficient presence the
family had continued to cohere in the decades since
my brother and I had left home. My father was a
more difficult personality, far less seductive and less
malleable, too: bluntly resisting points of view that
diverged only slightly from his own reigning biases
was, in fact, one of his most rigorously unthinking
activities. Still kneeling before him with his hand in
mine, I understood just how much we were going to
have to help him—what I couldn't understand was
how we were going to get through to him.

His obsessive stubbornness—his stubborn ob-
sessiveness—had very nearly driven my mother to a
breakdown in her final years: since his retirement at
the age of sixty-three, her once spirited, housewifely
independence had been all but extinguished by his
anxious, overbearing bossiness. For years he had believed he was married to perfection, and for years he

wasn't far wrong—my mother was one of those devoted daughters of Jewish immigrants who raised housekeeping in America to a great art. (Don't talk to anyone in my family about cleaning—we saw cleaning in its heyday.) But then my father retired from one of the Metropolitan Life's big South Jersey offices, where he'd been managing a staff of fifty-two people, and the efficient, clear-cut division of labor that had done so much to define their marriage as a success gradually began to be obliterated—by him. He had nothing to do and she had everything to do—and that wouldn't do. "You know what I am now?" he told me sadly on his sixty-fifth birthday. "I'm Bessie's husband." And by neither temperament nor training was he suited to be that alone. So, after a couple of years of volunteer work—stints at the V.A. Hospital in East Orange, with Jewish relief groups and the Red Cross—and even of working as an underling for a friend who owned a hardware store, he settled down to become Bessie's boss—only my mother happened not to need a boss, having been her own since her single-handed establishment of a first-class domestic-management and mothering company back in 1927, when my brother was born.

Just the summer before her death, during a weekend visit to Connecticut, when we two were alone having a cup of tea in the kitchen, she had announced that she was thinking of getting a divorce. To hear the word "divorce" from my mother's lips astonished me almost as much as it would have if she

had uttered an obscenity. But then the inmost inter-
twining of mother and father's life together, the difficulties and disappointments and enduring strains,
remain mysterious, really, forever, perhaps particularly if you grew up as a good boy in a secure, well-
ordered home—and simultaneously as a good girl.
People don't always realize what good girls we grew
up as, too, the little sons suckled and gurgled by
mothers as adroit as my own in the skills of nurturing
domesticity. For a very long and impressionable time
the male who's not around all day remains much
more remote and mythological than the palpable
woman of wizardly proficiency anchored firmly, during the decades when I was young, in the odorous
kitchen where her jurisdiction was absolute and her
authority divine. "But, Ma," I said, "it's late for a
divorce, no? You're seventy-six." But she was crying
quite pitifully already. That astonished me too. "He
doesn't listen to what I say," she said. "He interrupts
all the time to talk about something else. When we're
out, that's the worst. Then he won't let me speak at
all. If I start to, he just shuts me up. In front of
everyone. As though I don't exist." "Tell him not to
do it," I said. "It wouldn't make any difference."
"Then tell him a second time and if it still doesn't
work, get up and say 'I'm going home.' And go."
"Oh, darling, I couldn't. No, I couldn't embarrass
him like that. Not with company." "But you tell me
he embarrasses you when you're with company."
"That's different. He's not like me. He couldn't take
it, Philip. He would crumble up. It would kill him."

. . .

Three months after her death, in August 1981, I
came down from Connecticut to take him to the Jewish Federation Plaza in West Orange, where we were
to look at the living accommodations for retired and
elderly people. The Plaza had been recommended to
us by an old Newark friend of my brother's, a New
Jersey attorney on the Federation's board of direc-
tors. He had said he might be able to help my father
get an apartment without too long a delay, if my father was interested. The Plaza residents lived in two-
and three-room apartments of their own, but the
round of life itself was strongly communal: each evening they ate together in a dining room where
their meals were prepared for them, and they had
easy access to all the group activities at the flourish-
ing Y next door. West Orange was still one of Newark's pleasant suburbs, and the Plaza, as it was
described to me, was situated back on a green hillside overlooking a main thoroughfare, a few minutes'
walk from a shopping center and also from the Temple B'nai Abraham, which, like the Y, had been
transplanted from decaying Newark and served the
elderly as a cultural center as well as a synagogue.
In all, the Plaza struck me as a place where he would
not lack for companionship, and I was hoping that
after we had looked around, the idea of moving might
appeal to him. I was afraid that if he tried much
longer to hang on by himself in the Elizabeth apartment, he might literally die there of loneliness. His

meals, when he even sat down and ate them, seemed
to consist mostly of boiled hot dogs and Heinz baked
beans, and when I phoned in the middle of the day I
often found him asleep or in tears.

It was clear to me when I arrived at the apartment that day that he had been sitting there crying
by himself. He could have been crying since he'd got
up; for all I knew, he could have been crying all night
long. He'd spent a few weeks with us in Connecticut
in June and then again in July and had seemed in
that time to have gotten on top of the worst of his
grief, but now that he was back in the apartment
without my mother, he was hopelessly bereft all over
again. Though outside it was a beautiful August day,
he was sitting there with the shades down and no
lights on. I noticed that his clothes, while clean,
didn't quite match, as if getting out of bed he'd
pulled on whatever came to hand first. When I asked
what he'd had for breakfast, he answered, "Nothing.
Something. I don't remember."

"I've got a present for you." I turned on a light
and showed him my plastic shopping bag. "Just what
you always wanted. Close your eyes."

To my surprise he obeyed, like a child awaiting
a gift, though with no discernible look of anticipation
lighting up his face.

"Here." I produced from the bag a toilet bowl
brush and a bottle of Lysol that I'd bought at the
local general store before leaving Connecticut three
hours earlier. I'd also brought a bottle of 2 milligram

Valium. The idea was to get him off the 5 milligram tablets that I'd got for him after her death to help him sleep. "Come on," I said. "I'm going to teach you something you never learned at Thirteenth Avenue School."

He followed me into the bathroom, where several pairs of his big boxer shorts were hanging out to dry on a couple of wire hangers, and there I showed him how to clean the bowl with the brush.

"If you insist on being your own cleaning woman—" I began, but he cut me off abruptly.

"What do I need to pay somebody when I can do it myself? I get up at five and I begin vacuuming. I swore, I swore to myself when she died that I was going to keep this place the way Mother did." Those words alone got him crying again.

In the living room I gave him the new bottle of 2 milligram Valium and told him that if he needed it, he should now take one of these at night and pour the others down the drain. With this he didn't argue, though he was someone who previously would balk at the thought of taking even an aspirin. I was not so lucky when I reminded him that we were due at the Jewish Federation Plaza at one o'clock. He told me, dismissively, that he wasn't interested. "The hell with it," he said. "I'm fine right here. Everything is fine."

"Is it?"

"The hell with it, Phil—I don't want to go."

"Look, this isn't the way the game is played,

you know. You're not being fair. Instead of treating me like a member of your family, do me a favor and pretend you're still the manager of an insurance office. If somebody came to you at the Metropolitan with a proposal that he thought might be of help to you, you'd at least let the guy make his case. You'd sit back and hear him out, and then you'd think it over and come up with your decision. You certainly wouldn't say, after inviting him to talk to you, 'The hell with it,' and not even listen. I'm proposing to you only that we go up and look at the place, as we agreed we would a week ago. It is not a nursing home and it is not an old people's home or anything resembling one—it's a new apartment complex that people are lining up to get into and that's designed to make life comfortable and companionable for, among other people, men and women in your fix. It may be for you and it may not be for you, but there's no way for us to find out if you don't cooperate. Please, act like an insurance manager instead of whatever it is you *are* acting like, and maybe we can get something accomplished today."

It not only worked, my speech—it worked dramatically. "Okay!" he said with great decisiveness, and shot energetically up off the sofa. "Let's go."

I couldn't remember ever in my life persuading him to do something he didn't want to do. I wasn't sure that I'd ever before been so foolish as to try.

"That's more like it," I said. "Maybe you want to go in first and do something about your socks. You've got two different colors on. And I don't know

if that checked shirt goes with those plaid trousers.
You might want to change out of one or the other."

"Jesus," he said, looking down at his outfit,
"where am I?"

Though it was, as advertised, set back on a nice lawn
at the top of a rise overlooking Northfield Avenue,
the complex itself was not as homey and inviting as
I'd hoped. The Federation Plaza was new and in excellent repair but looked more institutional than res-
·idential, a cross between a small college dormitory
and a minimum-security prison. We were to be meeting with a woman named Isabel Berkowitz, a resident
who had volunteered to show us around. We had her
apartment number, but as the approach to the building was a maze of walkways, I stopped two very elderly women who were talking together on the main
path leading down to Northfield Avenue and asked if
they could direct us to Isabel Berkowitz's.

"My name is Berkowitz, also," one of them answered. She spoke with a Yiddish accent that, along
with her dress and her manner, made her appear to
have more in common with my grandparents' generation than with my mother and father and their
friends. I was pretty sure my father was thinking the
same thing—that he wasn't the kind of old person
these old people were and, what's more, he didn't
belong here. "I'm the other Berkowitz!" she told us
cheerily.

"Berkowitz from where?" my father asked her.

"Where else? Newark."

It was only a matter of seconds before he discovered that he had known her late husband, who had owned Central Paper Supply on Central Avenue, that she, in turn, had known his friend Feiner's brother, and so on.

In his apartment he had been sullen and angry, driving up to West Orange he'd been silent and grim, but he had only to come on someone who had known someone he had known in Newark to become blissfully self-forgetful—talkative, energetic, gregarious, very much the forceful insurance man whose years in Newark as an agent and assistant manager had familiarized him with nearly every Jewish family in the city.

Unmindful by now not only of his woes but even of what we were there for, he named for this other Mrs. Berkowitz all the shopkeepers whose businesses abutted her husband's Central Avenue store some forty years back.

I stood by till he had finished exhibiting to them his perfect memory and then I asked the old woman once again if she could tell us how to get to where we wanted to go. It turned out that she couldn't. When she tried, she became befuddled, all at once wholly unable to focus her mind. "Look," she said, after working hard to collect her thoughts, "I'm a pumpkin head—I'll *show* you where she lives."

The other woman didn't speak, and as they led us to the doorway opening onto Isabel Berkowitz's corridor, I saw that she was a stroke victim. My father noticed, too, and once again, without his even having to tell me, I heard him insisting that he wasn't this kind of old person. "True," I thought, "but given the kind of old person you are, what is going to become of you all alone?"

The Mrs. Berkowitz we were looking for was—to my relief—a quick-witted, lively, attractive woman who looked ten years younger than her seventy years. Her two-room apartment, though a bit cube-like, was bright with sunlight and the walls were hung with lots of little paintings she'd collected over the years. There was even one she'd painted herself, a colorful still-life, and framed alongside it were samples of her embroidery. She seemed delighted to see us, and immediately offered us something cold to drink, and within only five minutes of meeting her, when we two were momentarily alone again, my father turned to me and said, "She's some girl!" Though Isabel, who'd begun her career as a Brooklyn nurse and eventually became a public health administrator in New York, may have been a touch more worldly than my mother, her mixture of outgoing vitality and good-natured gentility reminded me very much of what my mother had been like when I was growing up. The resemblance could even have been what prompted my father—while we were waiting out in the corridor for Isabel to lock up her apartment and take us on a tour of the place—to announce spontaneously, as though all his troubles were over, "I love her! She's terrific!"

Isabel told us that she had moved in when the

Plaza first opened in October and that she was still having trouble "adjusting." It was a big change from her old life. She and her late husband—a vigorous, self-made man with a c.v. much like my father's— had lived in a spacious apartment in Jersey City with a view out to the Statue of Liberty. But she had decided to give it up and move to the Plaza because she had had a bad time with her health recently and 'because she wanted to be near the Berkowitzes.

My father surprised me by saying, "Yes, they're a wonderful family." He'd given no indication till that moment that he knew Isabel's Berkowitzes as *well* as the other woman's Berkowitzes. But then maybe he was only trying to ingratiate himself with a woman toward whom he seemed drawn by an undisguisable, surprisingly headlong tug of feeling.

As we were walking down the corridor, Isabel Berkowitz said to me, "So you're Philip Roth. Thank you for all the laughs." Turning to my father, she said, "Your son's got quite a sense of humor."

"The jokes," I told her, "originate with him."

"Yes?" She smiled and said to my father, "Tell me a joke, Herman."

She knew her man. "You hear the one about the two Jewish fellas . . . You hear the one about the fella who wakes up in the morning . . . You hear the one about the guy in Florida who gets sick . . ."

I hadn't seen him so animated in years, let alone since my mother's death. In fact, so busy was he presenting his Jewish joke repertoire, he barely bothered to look at the facilities that Isabel was beginning to show us. We walked through the dining hall, which was clean and simple, a large room that looked just like a school cafeteria; we peered through an open door into the kitchen, where the equipment was all shining and spotless and a heavyset black woman sat at a long table methodically cutting wedges of lettuce for several hundred dinner salads; we crossed over from the Plaza to the Y and looked into rooms where meetings were in progress and card games were going on, and though I kept hoping for him to begin to respond, if only with a little curiosity, to the life around him, and for him to see in it—if not necessarily now, in the days to come—a way out of his loneliness, his attention was riveted on Isabel, for whom he was now recounting stories, not entirely unfamiliar to me, about his childhood in immigrant Newark.

A day camp was in session at the Y, and when we went to look at the gym, there were some thirty little children sitting in a circle on the gymnasium floor, listening to their two counselors explain a new game. "Aren't our Jewish children beautiful?" Isabel said; but if she was trying to get him to see what was in front of his eyes, it didn't work—without even looking where she pointed, he continued describing Newark in 1912.

Only at the office of the director of the Y did the reminiscing momentarily abate while he told the director and his assistant there that the director of the

Elizabeth Y, where he was a morning regular several
times a week, was no damn good: the Elizabeth director never came into the health club to talk to the
men, he had no idea what was going on with them,
and, my father told them all bluntly, he himself
didn't get along with the man at all. "I don't even
bother with him. I organized the Roth Raiders, my
special little group of *alte kockers*, and we have a
good time on our own. The hell with him." "You're
the kind of person we need here," the director replied, but the veiled invitation elicited no response.
In the corridor outside the director's office, we ran
into Bleiberg, the president of the Plaza social orga-
nization, a man of about seventy-five suffering from
multiple sclerosis. Isabel introduced us. "Bleiberg.
Bleiberg. I remember you, Bleiberg," my father told
him. "You were a jeweler on Green Street." Bleiberg
had indeed been a jeweler on Newark's Green Street.
"How do you like living here, Mr. Bleiberg?" I
asked. "I love it," Bleiberg said, while my father
said, "Sure, Green Street. I'll tell you who else was
on Green Street," and did just that.

When we were back in the car later, I suggested
that we drive up the road to look at the shopping
center, where there was a bookstore and a bank and
a coffee shop and where, Isabel had told us, Plaza
residents sometimes went for lunch. Afterward, I
said, we could drive over to see the new B'nai Abraham.

"There's nothing to see," he said.

"But don't you want to take a look at the temple? You go in Elizabeth to Friday night services."

"Let's go home."

"Well," I said, after I'd turned down Northfield Avenue, in the opposite direction from the shopping center and the temple, "what did you make of it?"

"Nothing."

"Nothing at all?"

"Not for me."

"Well, you could be right. Though that's a first impression. Let it sink in a little. I hope you're going to take Isabel up on her invitation."

Isabel had suggested as we were leaving that he come back in a few days and together they go to one of the movies that were shown at the Y a couple of evenings each week. "I'll bring the popcorn," she'd said with a charming smile. The prospect had seemed to entice him at the moment and he'd taken her phone number and said he would call, but now, as though her proposal had been utterly preposterous, he told me, "Come on, I'm not driving all the way up here to go to the movies."

A calendar of the Y social activities for August and September, given him by the director, had slipped out of his hand and onto the floor of the car, but when we got back to Elizabeth, he didn't even bother to pick it up. For that matter, neither did I. Inside the apartment I went around raising the shades to let the light in while he went to the bathroom. Over the sound of his stream in the toilet bowl,

I heard him crying, "Mommy, Mommy, where are you, Mommy?"

He spent his first winter as a widower just north of Miami Beach in Bal Harbour, sharing the condominium apartment of his old friend Bill Weber. When I was growing up, Bill and his late wife Leah had lived not far from our Leslie Street apartment just across the Newark line in Irvington. In the early 1940s, along with their younger son, Herbie, who was my brother's age, they'd shared a small summer cottage at the Jersey shore with us and two other families, all of them friends of my parents going back to before the war. Bill had installed and serviced oil furnaces and may have been the only close family friend who was a skilled laborer as opposed to a salesman or a shopkeeper and who came home from work filthy at the end of the day. As a young Marine in World War I, Bill had been stationed at Guantánamo in Cuba, where he'd played the trumpet in the Marine band, and now, in his middle eighties, a little hard of hearing but otherwise quite fit, he maintained that he heard the tunes that he used to play with the Marine band being played inside his teeth. "That's not possible," my father told him categorically. "Herman, I hear it," Bill said. "I'm hearing it now." "You can't be." "I *am*. It's like in my mouth a radio is playing." I had flown from London to Florida to visit my father, and the three of us were sitting in their little kitchen, eating the bologna sandwiches that my father had prepared for lunch. "What do you hear exactly?" I asked Bill. "Tonight? 'The Marine Hymn,' " he said. " 'From the halls of Montezuma . . .' " he began singing. "You're imagining it," my father insisted. "Herman, it's as real as your Philip sitting in this kitchen."

My father appeared to me to have recovered all his old force and zest during his several months in Florida, and he looked wonderfully rejuvenated. Some years back, as a result of surgery, he'd lost the musculature in his midsection and developed a stomach, but otherwise he was, for his age, a most fit-looking man of medium height whose spontaneous, unassuming virility and spirited decency had made him instantaneously appealing to the widows around. He had been impressively strong through the arms and the chest when he was young, and a little of that solidity was still discernible in his upper torso, particularly so with this resurgence of vitality. Though he could be bluntly outspoken and dominate a conversation with his boiling anti-Republican diatribes, he happened to be an agreeable-looking person as well, and the mundane forthrightness his appearance exuded registered on all sorts of people as real charm. If he'd had the leisure for it, or the instinct, or the need, he might even have been handsome in an anonymous sort of way, but "handsome" was no asset where he'd fought his battles, and long ago he had settled upon looks people trusted rather than envied or praised. Now, of course, his hair was very thin and had only a touch of brown left in it; and his face, though unlined, had slackened along the jawline into the pronounced family dewlap; and his ears seemed somehow to have been tugged a bit, like taffy, and lengthened. Only his eyes, really, remained "beautiful," and you never would have known that unless you happened to be nearby when he slipped off his glasses for a moment. Then you would have seen how much gray there was in those eyes, and that there was even some green there—up close you would have seen how gentle and untroubled those eyes were, as though they alone had existed since 1901 beyond the reverberations of that crude, imperfect, homemade dynamo whose stubborn output had driven him through the obstacle course just about everything had been.

His Florida recovery may have owed something to his having found in Bill Weber a fairly good stand-in for my mother—a good-natured, even-tempered, untroublesome partner whose faults and failings he could correct unceasingly. I caught him improving Bill virtually the moment I arrived in Bal Harbour. When I got off the elevator on their floor, there were my father and Bill heading down the hallway together some twenty feet in front of me. Instead of calling out to them, I followed silently behind, listening while my father berated Bill for his social shortcomings. "Ask her to a movie, ask her out to dinner— don't just sit home night after night." "I don't want

to take her out, Herman. I don't want to take anybody out." "You're antisocial." "If that's what you
call it, okay, I am." "You live like a hermit."
"Okay." *"Not* okay. You've got to mix more with
people. There are women around here who are dying
for companionship. I'm not talking about women
with hang-ups. Not all of them want to possess you.
Not all of them want to sink their teeth into you." "I
don't want a woman. There's nothing I can do for a
woman. I'm eighty-six years old, Herman." "C'mon,
for Christ's sake, I'm not talking about that. I'm talking about eating a pleasant meal with somebody, so-
cializing with people like a human being." "You're
good at it, I'm not. I'll stay home." "I don't understand you, Bill. I don't understand why you fight me
like this when all I'm trying to do is to help you out."

The evening I arrived, a musical program was to
be performed by four residents of the condominium
who had formed a chamber ensemble earlier in the
season. The elderly Russian-born violinist, the ensemble leader, was said to be "Vienna-trained" by
the people my father had introduced me to at the
pool that afternoon. They had told me that if I liked
music I should be sure to come; the concert was to
take place following the weekly meeting of the Galahad Hall Social Club and would be attended by
nearly all those in Galahad Hall who were ambulatory
and even, as I would see, by some in wheelchairs
and on walkers who were accompanied by their
nurses. There was entertainment or a slide show or

a lecture every week, refreshments were served, and
I was assured that I would have a good time.

After our dinner of hot dogs and beans—prepared by my father while Bill neatly set three places
at the table—my father told Bill to put on a jacket
and a pair of shoes and come along with us to "the
musicale." All Bill wanted was to stay upstairs and
watch the pro basketball game on television, but as
my father wouldn't let up about Bill's failure to mix
with people, his failure to make friends, his failure
to go out in the evening and have a good time, Bill
gave in and agreed that he would come after the
music for the refreshments. But "after" wasn't good
enough, and ten minutes later, when my father still
wouldn't leave him alone, Bill pulled a jacket out of
the closet and put on a pair of shoes, and we took the
elevator to the social hall in back of the lobby, where
the meeting was already under way.

As the three of us came through the door, the
chairwoman of the Matzoh Fund, which collected do-
nations for Passover provisions for the Jewish poor
in South Miami Beach, was announcing the grand
total raised during the Matzoh Fund drive. The chairwoman looked down at her notes while she spoke,
causing several people around the room to shout,
"Can't hear you! We can't hear you, Belle!" When
she looked up, a little puzzled by the ruckus, a man
at the end of the back row, who must have been her
husband, put a hand to the side of his mouth and
called to her, "Pretend you're talking to me, honey

—holler." Everyone laughed, Belle loudest of all, and then in a good strong voice she announced that the fund had reached its goal of two thousand dollars, or the equivalent of about ten dollars from each person in the building, and the audience applauded.

I noticed two rows in front of us the people I'd met at the pool with my father that afternoon—the retired bathing suit manufacturer and his wife, the retired coffee and tea importer and his wife, and the recently widowed woman who years ago had been a New York buyer and was my father's choice as a mate for Bill Weber. All of them turned and waved hello as we slid into seats behind them. Our three seats in the last of the fifteen or so rows were virtually the only ones left in the house. Four music stands and four bridge chairs had been arranged in a little semicircle at the front, and off to the far side, near the door, was a long table set up for coffee. The refreshments were already there, the plates stacked high with cookies and slices of cake covered with Saran Wrap.

When the Matzoh Fund report was concluded, the club's president congratulated the chairwoman on the success of the drive. He was a dapper, suntanned man of about seventy—a passionate golfer, I'd been told that afternoon—who after his retirement as a successful leather goods and luggage manufacturer, had taken a desk at Merrill Lynch and made a second fortune managing his own money. He said, "Ladies and gentlemen. Before the music be-

gins, I want to tell you that a few moments ago a
young man walked in and I'd like to introduce him to
you. Young man, will you stand?"

I was just a year short of my fiftieth birthday but
he was pointing my way and I stood.

"Ladies and gentlemen, this is Philip Roth the
author, the son of Herman Roth."

They applauded, neither more nor less than they
had for the Matzoh Fund, and after acknowledging
the reception with a wave, I sat down.

But the president said, "Mr. Philip Roth, may I
ask you a question?"

I smiled at him and, coming halfway to my feet,
replied, "Oh, no questions, really. I'm just a guest."

"Just one question. Can you tell us a little bit
about your father?"

"I can assure you," I said, putting a hand on his
shoulder, "just ask my father and he'll tell you everything you want to know. Maybe even more."

My father got a kick out of that and so did his
friends in front of us. The retired bathing suit manufacturer turned around in his seat and said to him,
"The kid's got your number, Herm." At the pool
earlier in the day, he had jokingly referred to my
father as "the condo commander," but then, while
my father was in swimming, he had confided to me,
"Your dad's a real human being—he's the one here
who gives spirit to everybody else."

"One more question—" the president said.

I interrupted him: "Oh, you don't have to ask

me questions. I just came down to enjoy the music. Let the music begin!" And I got another round of applause and sat down again.

Bill, who was seated to one side of me, winked at me and whispered proudly, "That's telling 'em."

"You know me, Bill—always with the common touch."

"My Philip," Bill said, and he took my hand and sat there holding it in his even as the musicians appeared with their instruments, took their seats, and began tuning up. Bill wasn't holding my hand because he thought I was still seven but because he had known me since I was seven and he had a right to hold my hand, however old I'd become in the interim.

Over the next thirty minutes or so I came to understand—as I never entirely had when the performer was Perlman or Yo-Yo Ma—just how much muscular labor goes into playing a stringed instrument. In the middle of only the first movement I wondered if it was really a good idea for the viola player to go on. He was probably close to eighty, a large, heavyset man with a stern, expressionless face, and as the music heated up, that face grew paler and paler and I could see him beginning to pant. The performance was as alarming as it was heroic, as though these four aging people were trying to push free a car that was mired in the mud, and though the music didn't always sound like a Haydn string quartet, at the end of the first movement everyone applauded enthusiastically and some of the friends of the musicians shouted "Bravo! Bravo!" and half the audience got up and began to make their way toward the refreshment table.

"No, no!" the club president called out, jumping from the front row and turning to face the crowd. "Please, there's more!" The musicians, having mopped their faces and turned to a fresh page of the score, waited patiently until everyone was seated and quiet again. They weren't too many bars into the second movement, however, before the purses began clicking open and shut and couples began quietly gabbing together. Directly in front of me, a nicely dressed old woman who had a cane at her feet and a neatly stacked pile of bills on her lap was discreetly writing out checks and then clipping each check to the appropriate bill and putting it in an envelope. She had even brought along a roll of stamps. It was better than paying her bills upstairs alone.

Bill, with my hand still in his, inclined his head to my ear and whispered, "This stuff isn't for this audience, Philip."

"You may be right," I told him.

"A little Victor Herbert," he whispered, "a little Gershwin—a clarinet, an oboe, a French horn. This way all you hear is the screeching of the violin."

Twice more, at the end of a movement, many in the audience thought that it was over, and twice more, those who were headed for the coffee and cake had to be reprimanded and made to return to their

seats, and when the spirited finale finally came, and
it *was* over, really and truly over for good, they were
up on their feet to give a standing ovation that I
interpreted as a means of congratulating themselves
for their endurance as much as the musicians for
their physical fortitude. There had been something
sort of good-natured and self-disciplined about the
way they'd gone back to their chairs and sat there
that reminded me of people sitting through the
prayers in the synagogue when I was a kid—when,
after the reading of the Torah, the thing still went on
and on, and people had no idea what anyone was
reading but they sat there nicely *out of respect*. Of
course, there were always a few in the synagogue
who sat there on and on because they couldn't get
enough of it, but that didn't look to have been the
case at the musicale in Galahad Hall.

The club president was going from one musician
to the other, shaking each player's hand—the violist
could barely lift his head by then, let alone a hand,
and I continued to wonder if something medical
ought not to be done for him—and then the president
turned to the audience and waved both arms high in
the air, bidding us to clap even louder. "That's it,
ladies and gentlemen. Every artist, I don't care who
he is, needs to know if you like him or not. Let's let
them know how we feel!"

"Bravo! Bravo!" The applause had turned into a
rhythmic pounding with wild overtones of a kind you
couldn't have imagined emanating from this temper-

ate crowd, but their relief at being sprung was that great. The applause was loudest from those who had bounded out of their seats and were already lined up two deep in front of the refreshment table. "Bravo!"

On it went until, in a triumphant voice, the president announced above the tumult, "Ladies and gentlemen! Ladies and gentlemen! Good news! The artists are going to give you an encore!"

I thought there would be a riot. I thought plates would go sailing through the air from the direction of the refreshment table. I thought somebody might just walk up and put a foot through the cello. But no, these were decent people who had lived a long time, who had known and endured their share of grief before, Jewish people who had been born back when cultivation still had, even for untutored Jews, its religious clout, and so their deference to anyone who picked up a bow and a fiddle—as opposed to a bow and an arrow—was simply insurmountable. Agonizing as the prospect was, they kept their misery to themselves and returned yet again to their seats, many bearing coffee cups and cake plates, which they balanced on their knees or placed at their feet, while the first violinist's wife, a petite white-haired woman who had been sitting in the first row, stepped energetically out of the audience and sat down at a piano that was off to the side of the quartet. As the violist, the cellist, and the second violinist looked on in exhaustion, the first violinist, a man of the most remarkable stamina for his years, joined his wife in a duet by Fritz Kreisler. The violinist smiled at her whenever their eyes met, and this led several of the women around me to turn to each other and whisper admiringly, "He's looking at his wife."

My father had slept through most of the Haydn, but when the rousing encore was over, he popped up with everyone else and said, "Beautiful. Beautiful."

"Herman," Bill said to him, slowly rising from the seat beside me, "you were bored to death."

"Well, I'm not a music lover. But that doesn't mean it wasn't beautiful."

"It *wasn't* beautiful, Herman," Bill said unhappily. "It was awful. Jack Benny played better. I'm going upstairs."

"Jesus, Bill. Again? To sit with your ice cream and the television? Estelle is here," he said, pointing to where the ex-buyer could be seen talking animatedly to the first violinist's wife, who was at the piano still, playing something that nobody was listening to. The audience didn't dare to listen. They hadn't even applauded the encore for fear that it would unleash yet another one. "Talk to Estelle, will you?" my father begged Bill.

"Herman, I'm going upstairs."

"Bill, you're a grown man, you're eighty-six years old—you can talk to a woman."

But Bill, waving goodbye to me, headed for the refreshment table to get a piece of cake to take away in a napkin and have with his ice cream while he watched the game.

"What am I going to do with that guy?" my father asked me as we pushed into the throng at the
refreshment table.

"Why not nothing?" I suggested airily. "Why
not let him be?"

"So he can die on the vine of loneliness? So he
can sit there every night by himself? Absolutely not!"

He had found Bill to help and he had found women
to court, and the liaisons with these women, the sexual particulars of which I couldn't determine,
seemed as much the cause as the result of his reju-
venation. In just my first few days there he took me
for drinks at the homes of three wealthy Jewish widows ranging in age from sixty-five to seventy-five, all
of them quite polished and attractive and, according
to my father, eager to press on with their relation-
ship. Walking to their condominiums he would tell
me about the businesses their husbands had estab-
lished, how many children they had and what businesses the children had succeeded in, the state of
their health, the tragedies in their lives, how much
their apartments were worth, and then on the way
back home he would ask, "Well . . . what did you
think?" Each time I answered, altogether truthfully,
"She seemed very nice. I liked her." He'd then
reply, "She wants me to go on a cruise with her next
fall," or "You know what she tells me? Her apartment is twice what she needs. She rattles around

there all by herself. . . ." "And?" I would ask. "And nothing. Me, I just listen, I don't say nothin'. Phil, it's too soon. . . ." And here he would burst into tears, and though he didn't sob with the alarming abandon of those first months after my mother's death, the emotional flow was still considerable. "I didn't know how sick she was," he told me. "If I had had any idea . . ." "Nobody knew," I assured him. "There's nothing anybody could have done." "Oh, Bessie," he cried, "Bessie, Bessie, I didn't know, I didn't realize. . . ." Later, the two of us would go to dinner together, and after he'd drunk a vodka Gibson with his shrimp cocktail, I would suggest to him that it would be no crime if he went on a cruise in the fall with Cora B. or if he decided next winter to share the apartment of Blanche K., and he, in turn, would recount for me exemplary stories illustrating my mother's modesty, humility, loyalty, bravery, efficiency, dependability . . . and then we would walk back to the apartment, where Bill was watching television in his undershorts, and my father would start giving it to him for sitting all night by himself.

3

Will I Be a Zombie?

So, having arrived at his apartment from my mother's grave, I'd gone into the toilet, where, while eyeing my grandfather's shaving mug, I'd rehearsed my lines for the fiftieth time; then I'd come back out into the living room and looked at him slumped down in a corner of the sofa waiting for the verdict. Lil waited in the other corner of the sofa. She said to me, "Philip, do you want me to go?"

"Of course not."

"Herman," she said to him, "do you want me to stay?" But he didn't even hear her. And from then on Lil was so silent she might as well not have been there.

"Well," he said slowly, in a very gloomy voice, "what's the sad news?"

I sat in the chair across from him, my heart pounding as though I were the one about to be told something terrible. "You have a serious problem," I began, "but it can be dealt with. You have a tumor in your head. Dr. Meyerson says that given the location, the chances are ninety-five percent that it's benign." I had intended, like Meyerson, to be candid and describe it as large, but I couldn't. That there was a tumor seemed enough for him to take in. Not that he had registered any shock as yet—he sat there emotionless, waiting for me to go on. "It's pressing on the facial nerve, and that's what's caused the paralysis." Meyerson had told me that it was wrapped *around* the facial nerve, but I couldn't say that either. My evasiveness reminded me of his on the night my mother had died. At midnight London time, he had told me that my mother had had a serious heart attack and that I'd better make arrangements to fly home because they didn't know if she was going to survive. "It doesn't look good, Phil," he said; but an hour later, when I phoned back to tell him my flight plans for the next morning, he began to cry and revealed that she had actually died in the

PATRIMONY 67

restaurant where they had had dinner a few hours earlier.

"It's not Bell's palsy," he said.

"No. It's a tumor. But it's not malignant, and it's operable. He can operate, if we want him to. Dr. Meyerson wants to speak to you about an operation. I think it's a good idea to go back and talk to him now that we know what's up. I think that all of us should sit down together in his office and see if an operation is feasible. Finally, it's going to be your decision." I added, feebly, "Meyerson says that it's a routine operation." Meyerson had indeed used that phrase at the close of our phone conversation the day before—and I had thought, "Sure it is—routine for *you*."

"Will my face get better if he operates?"

"No. There just won't be any more deterioration."

"So, this is the way I'm going to be."

"I'm afraid so." Two minutes and I had learned to talk like a surgeon.

"I see," he said, and then he fell silent and then he was lost, alone and lost, and I wouldn't have been surprised if, right then, he had died. His eyes were looking out to nowhere, onto nothing, like someone who had just been fatally shot. He was gone like that for about a minute. Then, having absorbed the blow, he was back in the midst of the struggle, estimating the scale of his loss. "And my hearing?"

"What the tumor has damaged can't be re-

trieved. The operation, as I understand it, will prevent anything further from happening." Unless the
operation were itself to make something "further"
happen . . . but I didn't go into that. I would let
Meyerson apprise him of the risks, as well as of the
size of the tumor and the encasement of the facial
nerve.

"Will it grow back?" he asked.

"I don't know. I wouldn't think so, but you'll
have to ask the doctor. We'll make up a list of questions. You'll write them down and you'll take them
with you, and then you can ask the doctor everything
you want to know."

"Will I be a zombie?"

"I don't think Meyerson would propose the operation if he thought that could possibly be the outcome." But could it not be? Of the fifteen percent
who Meyerson allowed were worse after the surgery,
weren't they zombies or close enough to what my
father meant by a zombie?

"Where is it?" he asked.

"In front of the brain stem. That's at the base of
the skull. The doctor will show you where exactly. I
want you to write down all your questions so you can
go over everything with him on Monday. I've made
an appointment for us to see him and to talk this
thing through with him on Monday."

Of all things, he smiled, a wry half-smile really,
that worldly-wise, heartbroken smile that says, *But
of course.*

He put his hand to the base of his skull and, feeling nothing unusual there, smiled again. "Well, everybody leaves this earth in a different way."

"And," I replied, "everybody lives on it in a different way. Everybody's battle is different and the battle never ends. It's going to be an ordeal, but if the surgery seems to all of us the right way to proceed, then two months from now we're going to be sitting right here talking and you're not going to have that thing inside you pressing on those nerves."

It was wretched being unable to believe my own words but I did not know what else to say. I thought, "Two months from now he'll be in a convalescent home, barely able to lift a spoon to feed himself his cereal; two months from now he'll be a zombie in a bed somewhere, fed intravenously, whom I sit helplessly beside just the way he once sat with his father; two months from now he'll be in the cemetery where I wound up this morning."

In the meantime, he had gone off to the bathroom, and when he came out, trying with his hand to hide a large, damp urine stain on the inside of his trouser leg, he was talking about his appendectomy in 1944, when, against heavy odds, he had survived a dreadful bout with peritonitis. He was remembering how I had nearly died of a burst appendix and peritonitis in 1968. Then he was back in 1942, recalling my hernia operation at age nine—how he had taken me to see the family doctor after I had been in distress on a Sunday drive with the family. It was the second time in a month we had been to the doctor about my discomfort. "I told the doctor, I insisted, 'This boy is not a complainer, there must be something wrong,' and they told us there was nothing wrong, but I insisted and insisted and eventually they found out I was right. I told Dr. Ira, he should rest in peace—you remember our doctor, Ira Flax?" "Of course I do. I was nuts about him." "I said to him, 'Ira, this is a frisky boy who loves to run and play ball and if there is something wrong with him, I want it fixed.' I'll never forget him coming down those stairs in the Beth Israel Hospital the night that you were born. Three in the morning. The main staircase of the hospital. Ira was in his white gown. I said to him, 'What is it, Ira, Phyllis or Philip?' and he said, 'It's Philip, Herman. Another boy.' I'll never forget that. And my brother Charlie dying in my arms. Such a handsome man, all that energy, four children, and he died in my arms, my older brother I worshiped. And my Milton, my brother Milton—remember Milton?" "No," I said, "Milton died the year before I was born. That's how I got my middle name." "Milton," he said, "nineteen years old, a brilliant student, the shining light of the family, his senior year at Newark College of Engineering . . ." On and on, remembering the illnesses, the operations, the fevers, the transfusions, the recoveries, the comas, the vigils, the deaths, the burials—his mind, in its habitual way, working to detach him from the agonizing isolation of a man at the edge of oblivion and to connect his brain tumor to a larger history, to place his suffering in a context where he was no longer someone alone with an affliction peculiarly and horribly his own but a member of a clan whose trials he knew and accepted and had no choice but to share.

In this way did he manage to domesticate his terror and eat his lunch and that night, as he reported to me the next morning on the telephone, to get six continuous hours of sleep before waking in a sweat at 5:00 A.M.

I was not so lucky. I couldn't find *any* context to diminish my forebodings. The thought of his undergoing an operation as awful as that at the age of eighty-six was unbearable. And if he even made it successfully through the surgery, the prospect of the recovery—and if something *should* go wrong during the surgery . . . I couldn't sleep for six continuous minutes, and early the next morning, after sitting up in bed for several hours trying to read, I phoned my friend C. H. Huvelle, who until his retirement from practice a few years back had, as our family doctor in Connecticut, helped me through some physical difficulties of my own. I told C.H. about the brain tumor and the proposed operation.

"Look," he said, after hearing me out, "this is the way it stacks up. If he dies on the table, well, he will have died at eighty-six, which isn't the worst age to die at. If he lives and the operation is a success, which the guy says happens seventy-five percent of the time, good. The only bad result, as far as I see it, is if he suffers a further neurological deficit as a result of the surgery. Not the likeliest outcome, but it's possible and you have to calculate it in."

"I also have to calculate in what happens if we don't do anything. The brain surgeon assures me that it's going to get worse in a very short time. I take it that he means what you mean by further neurological deficit."

"That's what he means. Lots of things could go wrong."

"So," I said, "it could be agony either way. Operating could initiate one kind of horror and not operating another kind of horror."

"But operating," he said, "is more likely to yield something in the end that amounts to a *reprieve* from all-out horror."

"But I don't want to put him through this surgery for no good reason. It would be murder to come back from this kind of operation at forty; at eighty-six, it's unthinkable—isn't it?"

"Philip, get a second opinion, and then if you want to, call me back and we can talk it through some more. Just remember: you can't prevent your father from dying and you may not be able to prevent him from suffering. I've seen hundreds of people go through this with their parents. You were spared it with your mother and she was spared it, too. With him, it doesn't look like it's going to be so easy."

At about ten, after having tried a walk in Central Park to get myself to think about something else, I

phoned my father for the second time that morning.
"Zombie"—a word I don't suppose I'd heard since,
as children, my brother and I used to go to see horror
movies at the Rex Theater in Irvington—kept con-
juring up the most hideous medical scenarios, and
when I got back to the hotel, as disconcerted as when
I'd left for the park, I phoned to ask if he wanted to
go for a ride. I kept imagining him in the apartment,
sitting in the corner of the sofa, with the radio off
and the shades drawn—and when I did, it simply
made no sense for me to be strolling around New
York, or having lunch with a friend, or sitting in a
movie theater in order to forget for a few hours my
father and that massive tumor of his, over there together in Elizabeth, keeping each other company.

No, he didn't want to go for a ride.

But it was a beautiful spring day. We could drive
up to the Orange Mountains. We could go to Grun-
ings for lunch.

No, he was better off at home.

I said I would come over and we could take a
walk.

He didn't want to go for a walk.

I said I'd buy some lox and bagels and drive over
and have lunch with him and Lil at the apartment.
Was Lil around?

She was upstairs.

Well, tell her to come down and we'll have lunch
together.

It wasn't necessary.

"Maybe not for you," I thought, "but it is for me," and so I went out and bought lox, bagels, and cream cheese in a Sixth Avenue deli and then got the car and drove over to Jersey.

This time when I left the turnpike, I concentrated on my driving to be sure that I didn't mistakenly get onto the road to the cemetery. There was nothing to be gained by making a habit of that, though I wasn't sorry that the day before I had taken the wrong turn. I couldn't have explained what good it had done—it hadn't been a comfort or consolation; if anything it had only confirmed my sense of his doom—but I was still glad that I had wound up there. I wondered if my satisfaction didn't come down to the fact that the cemetery visit was *narratively* right: paradoxically, it had the feel of an event *not* entirely random and unpredictable and, in that way at least, offered a sort of strange relief from the impact of all that was frighteningly unforeseen.

When I got there, he was sitting as I had imagined, alone on the sofa, pitifully dejected-looking. The shades *were* drawn, the radio music *wasn't* on, and it appeared as though he hadn't even bothered to borrow yesterday's newspaper from one of his spendthrift neighbors. As I began to unpack the food I'd brought, he told me he wasn't hungry; when I suggested that instead of eating right away, we go out and take a walk, he made a noise to indicate that he didn't want to.

"Where's Lil?" I asked, turning on a lamp at about eleven in the morning.

"Upstairs."

"Don't you want to see her?"

He shrugged: he didn't care either way.

I hoped they hadn't argued, though I wouldn't have put it past him, even at the time of his greatest need, to go to work, first thing, on one or more of those many failings of hers that it had become his mission to eradicate. She ate too much and was over-weight; she was cheap and wouldn't part with a dime; she talked for hours on the phone with a sister of hers he couldn't stand; she was always running somewhere—to this flea market to buy crap, to that flea market to buy crap; she took stupid risks with money he told her to stick into CDs; she didn't drive a car to his satisfaction. . . . The list was long, maybe even endless, though of course, at the beginning of their affair, it had been for him as it is for all of us. In '82 and '83, when he was off for his second and third winters as a widower in Florida and she was still holding down her job in New Jersey, he had sent her a letter daily, by and large a miscellany of little news bulletins about his waking hours composed in fragments over the course of the day. They were sprightly, playful, conspicuously loving, shyly sexual, unashamedly romantic letters embellished on occasion with upbeat doggerel (both plagiarized and invented) and adorned with stick-figure drawings of the two of them holding hands, hugging and kissing, or lying side-by-side in bed, letters beginning "Sweet Lilums" and "Hello Baby" and "Dearest, dear Lil" —"a continus stream," as he, at once proudly and a

little self-mockingly, described his correspondence
to her, "of preaching, philosuphy, poems, and art."
And tenderness. "I hope," he wrote, "that winter is
not harsh, please take care going to and from work.
. . ." "Without you this is another dull day. . . ."
"Here's my hand to hold real tight. . . ." and directly
beneath, a third grader's drawing of a hand. "Think
of you all day. . . ." "I saw the smile on your pretty
face, when I called, also the happiness in your voice,
well, I must confess, I smiled also. . . ." "The song
the man is singing on the radio is 'Are you lonsome
tonight?' Are you? I was. . . ." Into a single, ordinary envelope, he stuffed, for her, Xeroxed copies of
the first pages of the sheet music for "Love Somebody," "Love Makes the World Go 'Round," "Love
Is a Many-Splendored Thing," "L-O-V-E," and
"Where Do I Begin" from the movie *Love Story*. In
precise detail he reported daily what he'd eaten, at
what time he'd swum and for how long, where he'd
walked and how far, whom he'd played cards and
kibitzed with, exactly how many days were left before he saw her again, even what he wore. "All
dressed in white, Shoes, socks, trousers, and shirt.
As for a Jacket, lets see. Either the red and white
one you say you don't care for or the black and white.
Well sweety I don't have you here to make the choice
so will have to make the momentous decision myselve. Tried them both on the red and white one
looks best on me. But decided on the other because
I will be sitting most of the time, and it is a lighter

weight, so that's that. . . ." Several times each week
he begged her to believe (apparently she didn't) that
the wealthy, charming widows he'd met his first winter in Florida were now only platonic friends he saw
very occasionally (which was only a shade away from
the truth), that she and she alone was his "pretty
lady," and, too, he kept her briefed on the day-by-
day struggle to broaden Bill Weber's horizons. "Bill
is a strictly Jewish meat and potatoes man, can't
even get him to go out for Chinese. . . ." "Finally
convinced Bill to go out for Chinese food. . . ."
There was absolutely nothing he didn't want to tell
her then. She had been perfect then, even her flaws
were beautiful. Yes, back then her physical propor-
tions were characterized in rather more flattering
terms than he would have used to describe them
now. "She's like that painter," he had told me, "you
know who I mean. . . ." I hadn't met Lil as yet, but
I took a guess. "Rubens?" "That's the one," he said.
"Well, *zaftig* is nice, too," I said. "Philip," he said
shyly, "I'm doing things I haven't done since I was a
boy." "We should all be so lucky," I told him.

But it wasn't her weight that had determined
Lil's fate so much as her docility, a patient, bovine
tolerance (or, for all I know, a saintly genius) for
being poked and prodded about her shortcomings.
There were times, to be sure, when the criticism
became too much even for her, and after a bitter
flare-up that took him completely by surprise, she
retreated upstairs and didn't return for a day or even

two. Then, thinking to himself, "Hell, I've got hundreds of women, I don't need her," he got on the phone to one or another of the widows down in Bal Harbour. There was also Isabel Berkowitz, up at the Jewish Federation Plaza, who had sometimes come to visit him when Lil was off on one of her biannual package tours with her sister, and whom he spoke with on the phone every week (and whenever he and Lil were on the outs). But the fact was that these women he phoned were wealthier and more worldly than Lil, women accustomed, as the widows of successful businessmen, to living somewhat more expansively than she ever had and capable of inspiring in my father rather more social admiration—in short, women less malleable than the woman he had settled on and ones whose faults he might not necessarily have got away with correcting a hundred times a day.

Lil, until her retirement—which my father had talked her into, somewhat against her better judgment—had worked in the office of an auto supply house that happened to be owned by one of my boyhood friends, Lenny Lonoff, whose family had lived just across the street from us when we were grade school kids. Lil had moved into my father's apartment building shortly after the death of her husband —and a year after the death of my mother—and lived there with one of her two stepsons, Kenny, whose financial acumen didn't entirely meet my father's standards. Not only didn't my father approve of how Kenny went about his business but he didn't

like the way Lenny Lonoff ran the auto supply house
either. When he told Lil as much, instead of retorting
that he didn't know what he was talking about or that
she didn't need his opinion, she sat and she listened
and didn't talk back, and as I see it, this forbearance
may perhaps have had more to do with what seduced
him than did the Rubenesque amplitude that he soon
came to see as a result of her continuing to eat much
too much despite his relentless upbraiding of her,
meal by meal, course by course, helping by helping.
Eating was her only revenge, and like the tumor, it
was something he could not stop, no matter how he
railed against it.

He could never understand that a capacity for
renunciation and iron self-discipline like his own was
extraordinary and not an endowment shared by all.
He figured if a man with all his handicaps and limitations had it in him, then anybody did. All that was
required was willpower—as if willpower grew on
trees. His unswerving dutifulness toward those for
whom he was responsible seemed to compel him to
respond to what he perceived as their failings as vis-
cerally as he did to what he took—and not necessarily mistakenly—to be their needs. And because his
was a peremptory personality and because buried
deep inside him was an unalloyed nugget of prehis-
toric ignorance as well, he had no idea just how un-
productive, how maddening, even, at times, how
cruel his admonishing could be. He would have told
you that you can lead a horse to water and you *can*

make him drink—you just hock him and hock him
and hock him until he comes to his senses and does
it. (Hock: a Yiddishism that in this context means to
badger, to bludgeon, to hammer with warnings and
edicts and pleas—in short, to drill a hole in somebody's head with words.)

After he and Lil got to West Palm Beach one
December, my father wrote a letter to my brother,
covering both sides of two sheets of white tablet
paper with his laborious scrawl. Sandy had cautioned
him, for the sake of domestic peace, to try to be a
little less critical of Lil, particularly about her eating,
once they were alone together in Florida. Sandy
added that he might want to take it easy, too, on
Jonathan, Sandy's younger son, who was just then
beginning to make the first real money of his life as a
sales rep for Kodak and whom my father, in weekly
phone calls and in letters, was advising, with the
usual relentlessness, to save and not spend.

Dear Sandy

I think there are two type's of (among people) Philos-
phies. People who care, and those that dont, People who
do and people who Procrastinate and never *do* or *help*.

I came home from the office and did not feel well,
you and Phil were very young. Mother made dinner. I did
not sit down to eat, instead I went into the liveing room.
Within the hour Dr. Weiss was in the house, mother
called him. This was the scenario. he asked me what was
wrong. I told him, I had a pain over my heart, after examination, he told me he could not detect anything wrong
with me. He then asked me what I did in excess. I told

him the only thing I could think of I smoke a lot, He said
how about cutting it down to three instead of 24 a day. I
said why not none and within the week my pain disappeared I cut out smokeing completely. *Mother cared, Dr.
Weiss advised, I listened,* There are many advisers in this
world, also people who *care* and *do,* and people who listen, In many instances lives are safed, and there are also
overindulgers, those who smoke to much and drink to
much, take drugs, and also are impulsive eaters. In each
case all these conditions can cause sickness and sometimes even worse.

You wanted a house. I went at once and got you the
money to buy it. Why? because I cared. Phil needed an
operation for Hernia, I took him to the Dr. and he was
operated on. Same with mother after she suffered for 27
years. Why because I cared and I am a doer. Did her
parents care, I guess so, but I felt the pain of both and
did, *I did not procrastinate.* I tell Jon and *hock him.* I use
all kind of Cliches , 'Like,' a fool and his money are soon
parted) (A Penny saved is a penny earned) (someday there
will be an old man dependent on you.) and when he asked
who, I tell him its you.) etc I dont tell him once, I keep
telling or Hocking, why, because he forgets, like a compulsive drinker, or drug taker, etc. Why do I continue,
hocking? I realize its a pain in the ass, but if its people I
care for I will try to cure, even if they object or
wont ^diceplin/disaplin themselves I including myselve . I have
many battles with my concience, but I fight my wronge
thoughts. *I care,* for people in *my way.*

Please excuse the spelling and writing. I was never a
good writer but now its worse, I don't *see so good*

> The Hocker, Misnomer
> it should be the carer
> Love
> Dad.

I will always continue to

Hock and Care. Thats me
to people I care
          for

"Did you and Lil have a fight?" I asked when I
walked in and saw him by himself.

"She's never around anyway, so what difference
does it make? She runs here, she runs there. When
she was sick, I took care of her, I waited on her hand
and foot. The hell with her. Let her go. I'm fine. I
don't need anyone."

"It's not my business to butt in," I said, "but is
this really a good time to start an argument?"

"I don't argue with anybody," he told me. "I
never argue. If I tell her something, I only tell it to
her for her own good. If she doesn't want to listen,
the hell with her."

"Look, put on a sweater and put on your walking
shoes, and I'm going to phone Lil, and if she wants
to come along, we're all going out for a walk. It's a
beautiful day and you can't sit around inside like
this, with the shades drawn and so on."

"I'm fine inside."

I then spoke four words to him, four words that
I'd never uttered to him before in my life. "Do as I
say," I told him. "Put on a sweater and your walking
shoes."

And they worked, those four words. I am fifty-

five, he is almost eighty-seven, and the year is 1988:
"Do as I say," I tell him—and he does it. The end of
one era, the dawn of another.

While he went to the closet and put on a bright
red sweater and his white Adidas, I phoned Lil and
asked if she'd like to take a walk with us.

"Your father's going for a walk?" she said.
"Really?"

"He is. Come and join us."

"I suggest we go out for a walk, that it'll do him
good, and he jumps down my throat. I don't mean to
criticize but that's the truth, Philip. You're the only
one he listens to."

I laughed. "And that may not last too long
either."

"I'll be right down," she said.

The three of us walked together to the drugstore
three blocks away, past the old apartment buildings
and the new condominiums that were going up where
the last of Elizabeth's opulent Victorian houses had
once stood. It was the same walk on which my
mother had overextended herself on the day she
died. Lil held him by one arm and I by the other,
since walking had become very uncertain for him
because of his poor vision. Only a few months earlier
he had been patiently waiting for the cataract on his
good eye to ripen so that it could be removed. Now,
instead of looking forward to the minor surgery
that would restore his vision and with it—he confi-
dently assumed—his robust independence, he was

contemplating an operation on his head that could kill him.

As we walked he began to reminisce in a very rambling way. "My memory is no good anymore," he explained.

But that wasn't exactly true. The sequence was often random and the focus sometimes blurry, but then, the logic of his recollections could always be a little elusive, even in the best of times. He certainly had no difficulty remembering the names of people dead now twenty, thirty, and forty years, or where they had lived, to whom they were related, and what they had said to him or he to them on occasions not necessarily that remarkable.

Through my father's mother's line we had belonged to a vast family network that had eventually organized into a family association in 1939, at the outbreak of the European war. While I was growing up, the association had consisted of some eighty families in and around Newark and some seventy families in and around Boston. There was an annual convention and an annual summer outing, a family newspaper that was printed quarterly, a family song, a family seal, and family stationery; a current roster of names and addresses of every family member was sent out to everyone each year, a Happy Day Fund looked after the ill and the convalescing, and an Education Fund assisted children of the family with their college tuition. In 1943, Herman Roth had become the fifth family member and the second of his brothers to be elected president. His first vice presi-

dent had been Harold Chaban of Roxbury, Massa-
chusetts. Harold Chaban was the son of Max Chaban
and Ida Flaschner—Harold's uncle was Uncle Sam
Flaschner, the family pioneer in America. His second vice president was Herman Goldstein, who lived
in New York. Goldstein was a hatter like Sender
Roth, loved to play cards with Liebowitz, and had
married Bertha, the niece who had lived with the
family on Rutgers Street when she came over with
her sister Celia from the old country in 1913. His
assistant treasurer had been his wife, Bess—my
mother—his assistant secretary had been his sister-
in-law Byrdine, Bernie's wife, his assistant historian
had been his younger sister, Betty. . . . All this was
recounted to Lil and me as we began our walk down
North Broad Street.

"Our family association," he said, "back in
those years, was one of the largest and strongest
associations of its kind in the United States." It was
the very tone in which he used to tell me as a boy
that Metropolitan Life was "the largest financial in-
stitution in the world." We may have been ordinary
people, but our affiliations were not without gran-
deur.

Out of nowhere, he said, "Used to be only Jews
around this part of Elizabeth when Mother and I
moved from Newark. Not when she was growing up
here, of course. It was Irishmen, then. All Catholics.
No more. Spanish, Korean, Chinese, black. The face
of America is changing every day."

"That's true," I said. "A friend of mine calls

Fourteenth Street in Manhattan the Fifth Avenue of the Third World."

"When my father sold the house on Rutgers Street," he said, "he sold it to an Italian family."

"Did he? How much did he get? What year was that?"

"I was born 1901, they moved to Rutgers Street 1902, we lived there fourteen years, so it must have been sold in 1916. Six thousand dollars, that's what he got for it. The Italian paid him in nickels, dimes, and quarters. It took a week to count it."

As we approached Salem Avenue, he gestured toward the apartment building on the corner. "That's where Millie used to live."

I knew that, of course; she and her husband, Joe Komisar, and my cousin Ann had moved there years ago, when I was in college. Millie was one of my mother's two younger sisters; she had died at seventy-eight only a few months earlier, and by pointing to her building he had been pointing not to where she used to live but to where she who no longer lived lived no longer. She and Joe were buried on one side of my mother, and my father's plot was on the other side. That's where Millie lived now.

"My father," he said, as we approached the drugstore to which my mother had taken the last long walk of her life, "my father had to beat my older brother Ed to prevent him from marrying a worldly woman. Had to beat him."

My Uncle Ed had been a bruiser with a short fuse who used to take me to football games when I

was a child. His big hands and his broken nose and
his rough, argumentative nature would thrill me for
an hour or two, and I loved him, but I was always
glad, at the end of a day's outing, that he was my
cousin Florence's father. "You never told me that,"
I said. "Grandpa beat him?"

"Had to. Saved him. Saved him from that
woman."

"How old was Ed?"

"Twenty-three."

He'd first told me that story when I was sixteen
and in my last year of high school. I don't remember
why he told it, but it was at dinner, near the end of
the meal, and I had jumped up from the table in a
rage and then bolted from the room when I'd heard
him conclude, "They don't have that kind of discipline anymore." My mother had come into my bedroom to try to get me to go back to eat my dessert;
she had begged me to forgive him for whatever he
had said that offended me so. "Please, dear, do it for
me. Your father is not an educated man. . . ." But I
had been adamant and refused to return to spoon
down Jell-O across the table from somebody who
considered beating the love for a woman out of a
twenty-three-year-old man—even one as pigheaded
as my Uncle Ed—a praiseworthy form of discipline.

No doubt he had forgotten that incident and so,
actually, had I, until the moment, thirty-nine years
later, when for some obscure reason he had chosen
to tell this story to me again.

But there was no rage now against the story-

teller. It was I, in fact, who now said to him, philo-
sophically, "Well, they don't have that kind of
discipline anymore."

"No. My brother Bernie, he should rest in
peace, you know what he said to me when I told him
not to marry Byrdine Bloch? Of course I was proved
right, because after twenty years of marriage and two
beautiful children, he wound up getting that terrible
divorce that tore the family apart. But when I cautioned him about Byrdine, when I told him, 'Bernie,
she looks old enough to be your mother—is that
really what you want?' you know what he said to me,
an older brother who was trying only to warn him?
'Mind your own goddamn business.' We didn't talk
for months."

"That was when?" I asked.

"That? That must be . . . 1927. I married
Mother in February and Bernie married Byrdine in
July."

"I didn't realize that you were both married in
the same year," I said.

We were walking back now the way we'd come.
He was silent for a while. Then, as though having
glimpsed the solution to some intractable problem
after a long and arduous effort, he began to say, "Yes
. . . yes . . ."

"Yes what?" I asked.

"I've been alive a long time."

"You're the insurance man, you know the statis-
tics. On the actuarial charts you have achieved a
great age."

"Where is the tumor?" he asked for the second time in two days.

"In front of the brain stem. At the base of the skull."

"Have you seen the pictures?"

I didn't want him to think that too much had been going on without his knowledge and so I lied. "I couldn't read them if I had," I said. "Look, it's operable—remember that." But that was what he couldn't forget, and dreaded most. "If we all decide that's the course to follow, then he'll go in and get it out, and after a brief convalescence, you'll be yourself again."

"It would be nice to have a few more years," he said.

"You'll get them," I said.

I drove over again on Sunday morning and he had a set of sherry glasses ready for me to take away, each glass individually wrapped in a page of the previous week's Sunday *Star-Ledger* and all of them wedged bulkily together in a shoebox. He never used them, he said, he didn't need them, and he wanted Claire and me to enjoy them in the country.

Ever since my mother's death, each time he came to stay with us in Connecticut he had something with him in a paper bag or a shopping bag or in the little plaid valise that he carried alongside him during the three-hour car ride with the local driver we sent down to Elizabeth to get him. Unlike the

sherry glasses, it was usually a present for him and
my mother from me, or from Claire and me, that
now, years later, he was returning as though what
they had been given had only been on loan or left
there in storage. "Here are those napkins." "What
napkins?" "From Ireland." Ireland? That would
have been 1960, the year of my Guggenheim. My
then wife and I had stopped in Ireland on the way
home, to walk around Joyce's Dublin. "There's a
tablecloth, too," he added, "from Spain." 1971. Gau-
dí's Barcelona. Or, "Here are the place mats. I don't
think Mother used them twice. For her, they were
special, for company only." "Here are the steak
knives" and "Here is the flower vase" and "Here are
the coffee mugs," and in the beginning, when I re-
sisted, explaining to him, "But they're yours, they
were gifts," he would reply, with no idea that there
might be a grain of insult lurking in all this unburden-
ing, "What the hell do I need them for? Look at this
clock. A beautiful clock that somebody gave us.
Must have cost a fortune. What good is it to me?"

The clock had cost about two hundred dollars in
Hungary in 1973. I had given it to my mother, a little
porcelain clock with a floral design of the kind she
liked that I bought for her in an antique shop in
Budapest, on my way home one spring from visiting
friends in Prague. But I took it back silently. Little
by little I took everything back, struck each time by
how inconsequential to him was the sentimental
value—even the material value—of things intended

to betoken the love of those he most cherished.
Strange, I would think, to find that particular blank
spot in a man on whom the claims of family were so
emotionally tyrannical—or maybe not strange at all:
how could mere keepsakes encapsulate for him the
overpowering force of blood bonds? Item by item, I
took it all back like a well-trained refund clerk in a
first-rate department store, but wondering if perhaps
what he was thinking, while he wrapped these gifts
in old newspaper and stuffed them in cartons of
every description, was that this way we wouldn't
have too many of his possessions to bother about
after the funeral. He could be a pitiless realist, but I
wasn't his offspring for nothing, and I could be pretty
realistic, too.

This time, instead of silently accepting the
goods being returned, I reminded him that I was still
a transient in a New York hotel, didn't know when
I'd next be in Connecticut, and would just as soon
have him hold on to the glasses.

"Take them," he insisted. "I want to get rid of
them."

"Dad," I said, setting the shoebox on the breakfront, where I assumed the glasses had been stored
all these years, "these glasses are the least of our
worries."

But rushing around the apartment looking for
the next thing to get rid of, finding the glasses, pack-
ing them in newspaper, finding the shoebox—for a
moment this had given the day a purpose, provided

some little release for all that was brutally thwarted. Now there was nothing for him but to be frightened again. I was sorry, suddenly, for not having let him have his way and just taken the damn things back to the hotel. But I was getting frazzled, too.

"I've been like that all my life," he said, dropping unhappily onto his spot on the sofa.

"Like what?"

"Impulsive."

I was unused to hearing this kind of self-criticism from him, and I wondered if it was such a wonderful development. At the age of eighty-six, with a massive tumor in his head, better to continue wearing, at either side of his bridle, those blinders that had kept him pulling his load straight ahead all his life.

"I wouldn't worry about it," I said. "It isn't as if you're only impulsive. You can be cautious and prudent, too. You oscillate. People do."

But he was being gnawed at by something and wouldn't be consoled.

"What are you thinking?" I asked.

"I gave my tefillin away. I got rid of my tefillin."

"Why?"

"They were sitting in the drawer."

Tefillin are the two small leather boxes containing brief Biblical extracts that an Orthodox Jew fastens to himself by narrow thongs—one box strapped to the forehead, the other to the left arm—during his weekday morning prayers. Back when my father was an overworked insurance man, being a Jew for him hadn't had much to do with formal worship, and like most of the first-generation American fathers in our neighborhood, he visited the nearby synagogue only on the High Holidays and, when it was necessary, as a mourner. And at home there were really no rituals he observed. Since his retirement, however, and particularly in the last decade of my mother's life, they had begun to attend services together mostly every Friday night, and though he still didn't go so far as to lay tefillin in the morning, his Judaism was more pointedly focused on the synagogue and the service and the rabbi than it had been at any time since his childhood.

The temple was a hundred or so yards down the road on a little side street off North Broad, in an old house that was rented by the small congregation of elderly, local people, who were barely able to meet the upkeep costs. To my surprise—and perhaps because they couldn't afford anyone else—the cantor wasn't even a Jew but a Bulgarian who worked for a New York auction house during the week and for this little conclave of Elizabeth Jews on their sabbath. After the service was over, he sometimes entertained them with songs from *Yentl* and *Fiddler on the Roof*. My father loved the Bulgarian's deep voice and considered him a buddy; he also thought highly of the yeshiva student who came over from New York to lead their services on the weekend, a twenty-three-year-old whom my father called "Rabbi" most respectfully and spoke of as something of a sage.

However humble their manifestations, these

yearnings for a formalized religion in his old age were inspired by something far from hypocrisy or conventional decorum; in fact, the consolation that he seemed to derive from going to synagogue regularly —the sense of unity it bestowed on his long life and the communion with his own mother and father he told me he felt there—made his "getting rid" of the tefillin one of the more enigmatic instances of his lifelong habit of relinquishing, rather than saving, the treasured objects of the past. Given the link of sentiment that Jewish belief now seemed to furnish between the isolation of old age and the striving, populous life that was all but gone, I could have imagined him, instead of parting with his tefillin, rediscovering in the mere contemplation of them something of their ancient fetishistic power.

But my imagining this old man meditatively fondling his long-neglected tefillin was so much sentimental kitsch, really, a scene out of some Jewish parody of *Wild Strawberries*. How my father actually disposed of the tefillin reveals an imagination altogether bolder and more mysterious, inspired by a personalized symbolic mythology as eccentric as Beckett's or Gogol's.

"Who'd you give the tefillin to?" I asked him.

"Who? Nobody."

"You threw them out? In the trash?"

"No, no, of course I didn't."

"You gave them to the synagogue?" I didn't know what you did do with tefillin when you no longer wanted or needed them, but surely, I thought, there would be a religious policy for discarding them, overseen by the synagogue.

"You know the Y?" he said to me.

"Sure."

"Three, four mornings a week when I could still drive over there, I'd swim, kibitz, I'd watch the card game. . . ."

"And?"

"Well, that's where I went. The Y. . . . I took the tefillin in a paper bag. The locker room was empty, I left them. . . . In one of the lockers."

The halting way he revealed the details, the bafflement he himself seemed to feel looking back now on this original plot he'd devised for their disposal, prompted me to wait a little before asking anything further.

"I'm curious," I finally said. "How come you didn't go to the rabbi? Ask him to take them off your hands."

He shrugged and I realized that he hadn't wanted the rabbi to know what he was up to, for fear of what the twenty-three-year-old whom he so respected would think of a Jew who was ditching his tefillin. Or was I wrong about that, too? Maybe he'd never even thought of the rabbi, as perhaps the shrug was meant to indicate—maybe it was just revealed to him in a flash, the knowledge that in that secret place where Jewish men stood unashamedly naked before one another, he could lay his tefillin to rest

without worry; the understanding that where his tefillin would come to no harm, where they would not
be profaned or desecrated, where they might even
be resanctified, was in the midst of those familiar
Jewish bellies and balls. Perhaps what the act signi-
fied was not his shame before the young rabbi-in-
training but a declaration that the men's locker room
at the local YMHA was closer to the core of the
Judaism he lived by than the rabbi's study at the
synagogue—that nothing would have been *more* artificial than going with the tefillin to the rabbi, even
if the rabbi had been a hundred with a beard down
to the ground. Yes, the locker room of the Y, where
they undressed, they schvitzed, they stank, where,
as men among men, familiar with every nook and
cranny of their worn-down, old, ill-shapen bodies,
they kibitzed and told their dirty jokes, and where,
once upon a time, they'd made their deals—that was
their temple and where they remained Jews.

I didn't ask why he hadn't turned them over to
me. I didn't ask why, instead of giving back to me all
those napkins and tablecloths and place mats, he
hadn't given me the tefillin instead. I wouldn't have
prayed with them, but I might well have cherished
them, especially after his death. But how was he to
know that? He probably thought I would have scoffed
at the very idea of his handing on his tefillin to me—
and forty years earlier he would have been right.

I didn't ask because I realized that to do so was
truly to place the two of us back inside that corny

scenario I couldn't seem to cut myself loose from. Somewhat improbably, where his tefillin were concerned, it was I whose imagination kept running to the predictably maudlin while his had the integrity of a genuinely anomalous talent, compelled by the elemental feeling that can lend ritualistic intensity to even the goofiest act.

"Well," I said, when it was clear that he had no more to tell me, "one of your pals there must have got a big surprise when he came up from the pool. He must have thought a miracle had happened. There he had left his shower clogs in the bottom of his locker and, lo and behold, they'd been turned into tefillin. An argument not only for the existence of God but for the existence of a God most bountiful."

He didn't as much as smile at what I'd said— maybe because he didn't get it, or maybe because he did. "No," he replied, in all seriousness, "the locker was empty."

"When did you do this?"

"In November. A couple days before we went to Florida."

So—he had more than likely been thinking *this*: "If I die in Florida, if I never come back . . . no, the tefillin must not wind up in the garbage."

"Then, November thirtieth, we flew to West Palm. I carried my suitcases from the baggage place all the way to the taxi stand—that's how good I felt. And the next morning, my first morning in Florida, I woke up and this had happened in my sleep." Yet again he was pushing the fallen cheek up with his fingertips to see if this time it would stay. "I look in the mirror, I see my face, and I knew my life would never be the same. Come here," he said, "come to the bedroom."

I followed him down the corridor from the living room, past the blown-up photographs of my brother's sons, taken some twenty-five years ago, when they were little children vacationing on Fire Island. Why he hadn't thought to give Seth or Jonathan the tefillin was easier to understand than why he hadn't thought to pass them on to me. My nephews, raised in a secular ethos, with no knowledge of Judaism, were Jews in name alone; my father, like my mother, adored them, worried about them, praised them, lavished on them gifts of money—and a good deal more advice than they wished to hear—but he knew better than to expect them to know what the tefillin were, let alone to want to own them.

As for my brother, my father probably imagined that Sandy would have been as unreceptive as I to such a bequest, though my guess is that Sandy might have been touched by that memento, not because of its religious significance but as a solid piece of our past, as something that he remembered, as I did, seeing neatly stored for years and years in a velvet bag in a drawer of the dining room breakfront in the apartment where we had grown up. But our father, being our father, couldn't have been expected to understand that. He understood, like the rest of us,

only what he understood, though that he understood
fiercely.

I could no longer enter my father's bedroom without
remembering the night just after my mother's death
—and after I had arrived from London that afternoon
—when I had slept with him in his double bed. Sandy
and Helen had gone to sleep at Sandy's suburban
house in Englewood Cliffs, where Seth and Jon, now
young working men, were still living but which Sandy
planned to sell shortly, since his job had already re-
located him in Chicago.

In May 1981, at seventy-nine, my father was in
excellent health and impressively vigorous, but
twenty-four hours after his wife died in that seafood
restaurant, he looked almost as bad as he did now
disfigured by the tumor. That first night together,
before bed, I had given him 5 milligrams of Valium
and a glass of warm milk to wash the tablet down.
He disapproved of tranquilizers and sleeping pills,
criticized vehemently anyone who relied on either—
instead of on willpower the way he did—but beginning that night and for the next few weeks, he accepted the Valium without any questions when I said
it would help him to sleep (though later, perhaps to
ease his conscience, he referred to the drug he'd
taken as Dramamine). We took turns in the bathroom
and then, in our pajamas, we lay down side by side
in the bed where he had slept with my mother two

nights before, the only bed in the apartment. After
turning off the light, I reached out and took his hand
and held it as you would the hand of a child who is
frightened of the dark. He sobbed for a minute or two
—then I heard the broken, heavy breathing of someone very deeply asleep, and I turned over to try to
get some rest myself.

Thirty minutes later, having taken no Valium, I
was lying there wide awake, when, on the night table
beside me, the phone rang. I grabbed it so that my
father's sleep wouldn't be disturbed and heard someone laughing at the other end. "Who is this?" I
asked, but the answer was more crazy laughter. I
hung up, uncertain whether the call was a fluke
wrong number or deliberate, the work of some ghoul
who followed the obituary pages in the local paper
(where my mother's death had been reported that
morning) and then phoned the families of the dead at
night to get his kicks. When the phone rang again
less than a minute later—the luminescent clock
radio still showed eleven-twenty—I knew it was no
innocent wrong number. There again was the vicious
laugh of one who has triumphed over an enemy, the
gleeful sadism of a victorious avenger.

After putting down the receiver, I got out of bed
and ran to the living room extension to take the receiver there off the hook before the phone rang a
third time. I left it like that until around six the next
morning, when I got up and stole back into the living
room to replace it so that my father wouldn't ask any

questions. I was in the bathroom when it rang around
seven. My father answered. When I came out and
asked who had phoned so early, he said angrily, "No
one," but it was clear enough what had happened.
"Who was it?" I repeated, and this time he described
the laughing he'd heard. "Sounds like some screw-
ball," I told him, without mentioning the calls I'd
taken the night before. "It's Wilkins," he replied.
"Who's Wilkins?" "From across the street." "How
do you know it's him?" "I know, all right." "What's
he got against you?" I asked. "He's a fascist dog. A
real Jew-hater. He lives alone. Not a friend in the
world. Just that mutt. Loves only Mr. Ray-gun and
Plastic Nancy and that filthy mutt of his. Put Ray-
gun stickers all over the laundry room. *Our* laundry
room. Doesn't ask—just comes over here and does
it." "So you told him not to." "I saw them, and sure,
I told him not to. And the next day he puts up more.
When I saw what he'd done, I tore 'em down. I
phoned him. I told him that wasn't what this laundry
room was for. It was for people to wash their clothes
in peace and not for political campaigning." "What
else did you tell him?" "I told him what I thought of
Mr. Ray-gun. I told him, in case he hadn't heard,
just what Jews have suffered for two thousand
years." "You're sure it's him?" "It's Wilkins, all
right. I'll get him," he said, half to himself, "I'll get
the son of a bitch." "Dad, don't bother—from the
sound of it, they got him. You know what a punish-
ment it is for a man to laugh at somebody else's grief?

Forget him. Let's just get ready now—we've got a big day."

We buried my mother at noon, he began emptying out her bedroom closet and her bureau drawers around one, and by ten-thirty we were back in the double bed—and at eleven-twenty, while my father slept and I lay there wide awake once again, wondering what was going to become of him and wondering where my mother was, the phone rang. The laughing began as soon as I picked it up. I listened for a long time with the phone held tightly to my ear. And then, when the caller had neither stopped laughing nor hung up, I said softly—doing my best, by cupping the mouthpiece, not to wake my father—"Wilkins, pull this shit one more time, *once* more, and I will be over at your door with my ax. I've got a big ax, Wilkins, and I know where you live. I will beat your door down with my ax and then I am going to come in and split you up the middle like a log. Do you have a dog, by any chance? I'm going to turn your doggy into sausage, Wilkins. With just my ax to help me, I will then shove him up your ass and down your throat until you and Fido are one. Call my father one more time, day or night, *ever again*, and your head, you crazy, sick, psychotic ghoul, your fucking head, when I am finished with it . . ."

My heart was pumping blood as though for ten people and my pajamas were soaked through with the perspiration of someone who has lain all night in a malarial fever and, at the other end, the phone was dead.

. . .

In the bedroom—where the mahogany bedroom suite no longer gleamed with polish as it had when my mother was in charge of the housekeeping, where instead you could now initial the dust coating the upper surfaces—my father showed me, in the middle of the top bureau drawer, the little metal box where he kept his will, his insurance policy, and his savings books. There was also a record of his CDs and municipals. "All my papers," he said. "And here—the key to my safe deposit box."

"Okay," I said.

"I did what you told me," he said. "I made all my savings accounts joint with Sandy."

He took out the savings books—there were four of them—to show me where my brother's name now appeared beneath his as the account owner. Flipping through the savings books, I saw that the savings added up to about fifty thousand dollars; the CDs and municipals came to another thirty thousand—they, too, were to be left to my brother.

"The ten-thousand-dollar insurance policy goes to you," he said. "I know what you told me, but that I had to do—I wasn't going to leave you nothing."

"Fine," I said.

When I was visiting him in Florida some two or three years after my mother's death, the subject of his will had come up and I had told him to leave all his money to Sandy to split, as he wished, between his two kids and himself. I told him that I didn't need any money and that what Seth and Jonathan got could make a big difference to them if the money was divided two ways, or three at the most. I had meant it when I said it, I had confirmed it in a letter to him afterward, and I hadn't thought about his will since.

But now with his death anything but remote, being told by him that he had gone ahead and, on the basis of my request, substantially eliminated me as one of his heirs elicited an unforeseen response: I felt repudiated—and the fact that his eliminating me from the will had been my own doing did not at all mitigate this feeling of having been cast out by him. I had made a generous gesture that was also, I suppose, of a piece with the assertions of equality and self-reliance that I had been making to my father since early adolescence. Admittedly, it was also a characteristic attempt to take the moral high ground within the family, to define myself in my fifties, as I had in college and graduate school and later as a young writer, as a son to whom material considerations were largely negligible—and I felt crushed for having done it: naive and foolish and crushed.

To my great dismay, standing with him over his last will and testament, I discovered that I wanted my share of the financial surplus that, against all odds, had been accumulated over a lifetime by this obdurate, resolute father of mine. I wanted the money because it was his money and I was his son and I had a right to my share, and I wanted it because it was, if not an authentic chunk of his hard-

working hide, something like the embodiment of all
that he had overcome or outlasted. It was what he
had to give me, it was what he had wanted to give
me, it was due me by custom and tradition, and why
couldn't I have kept my mouth shut and allowed what
was only natural to prevail?

Didn't I think I deserved it? Did I consider my
brother and his children more deserving inheritors
than I, perhaps because my brother, by having given
him grandchildren, was more legitimately a father's
heir than was the son who had been childless? Was
I a younger brother who suddenly had become unable to assert his claim against the seniority of someone who had been there first? Or, to the contrary,
was I a younger brother who felt that he had en-
croached too much upon an older brother's preroga-
tives already? Just where had this impulse to cast off
my right of inheritance come from, and how could it
have so easily overwhelmed expectations that I now
belatedly discovered a son was *entitled* to have?

But this had happened to me more than once in
my life: I had refused to allow convention to determine my conduct, only to learn, after I'd gone my
own way, that my bedrock feelings were sometimes
more conventional than my sense of unswerving
moral imperative.

During the walk we took that afternoon, in which
I steered my father very slowly twice around the
block, I was not able to tell him, however much I
wanted to—and however efficaciously humbling a

confession of error might have been—that I would
like him to reassign to me the share of his estate that
he had originally bequeathed to me in his will. For
one thing, because several years back my brother
had had to provide his signature to gain access to the
joint savings accounts, he already knew of the
changes, and it did not seem worth even the thirty or
forty thousand dollars to establish the conditions for
a family feud or the eruption of poisonous feeling that
is notoriously associated with the last-minute adjust-
ment of an inheritance. And there was my pride—if
you like, the hubris. In short, for something like the
reasons that had probably contributed to my telling
him to leave the money to others in the first place, I
now found myself unable to renounce my instruc-
tions.

So much for learning from one's mistakes. "Let
it be," I thought. "It's almost worth the dough to be
able to savor, yet again, the comedy of your own
automatic brand of elevated stupidity."

But if it was too late—or for me just too difficult
—to lay claim to my original share of the money, I
knew what it was I wanted in its place. But I then
discovered myself unable to ask for *that*. Not directly, anyhow. Self-reliant to the last! Independent
to the end! The son perpetually protesting his auton-
omy! *I don't need anything.*

"Tell me about Grandpa's shaving mug," I said.
"I was looking at it in your bathroom. Where was his
barbershop? Do you remember?"

"Of course I remember. Bank Street. Below Wallace Place, where the German hospital used to be, on the corner of Wallace Place and Bank Street. There was a barber on Bank Street and when I was a little boy we used to go around and get my hair cut and my father would get a shave. The mug had 'S. Roth' and a whaddyacallit on it, a date, and they kept it for him in this barbershop."

"How'd you come to get it?"

"How did I get it? That's a good question. Let me remember. I don't think I did. No. I didn't. I took it from my brother Ed. Yes. When we moved from Rutgers Street, Pop took it with him to Hunterdon Street and went to the barber on Johnson Avenue and Avon Avenue and then Ed took it after Pop died and I took it from him. I think it was the only thing that was ever left to me. And it wasn't even left to me. I took it."

"You wanted it," I said.

"I wanted it," he told me with a laugh, "since I was a little boy."

"Want to know something?" I said. "I did, too."

He smiled at me with the half of his mouth that could still move. "Remember when we came to visit you in Rome, me and Mother, when you took me for a shave?"

"That's right. On Via Giulia, in that tiny barbershop. That may have been the best of that whole year for me," I said, thinking of the marital battles that erupted daily in the small apartment, around the cor-

ner from Via Giulia, on Via di Sant' Eligio, that I
shared unhappily with an unhappy wife when we
were living in Italy on my thirty-two-hundred-dollar
Guggenheim. "I'd go down the street for a shave in
the afternoon after I'd finished writing. My big luxury. The barber was Guglielmo. He wanted to talk
all the time about Caryl Chessman. He prided himself on his English. Every time I came in, 'Happy
birthday, Maestro, Fourth of July.' Hot towels, big
shaving brush, straightedge razor, slapped silly with
witch hazel to top it off, and all for the equivalent of
about fifteen cents. 1960," I said. "You would have
been only a couple of years older than I am now."

"I used to go get a shave with Bill Eisenstadt,
he should rest in peace. Remember Bill?"

"Of course. Bill and Lil and their son, Howie."

"A barber on Clinton Place, right around the
corner from the high school. Cost a quarter. You
leave it to Bill to find the last quarter shave in Newark."

From Bill Eisenstadt he went on to invoke Abe
Bloch and Max Feld and Sam Kaye and J. M. Cohen,
the totemic male figures out of my earliest childhood,
insurance men with him at the Metropolitan, pi-
nochle players in our kitchen on Friday nights, com-
panions, with their wives and kids, on the Memorial
Day picnics up at the South Mountain Reservation—
the veteran foot soldiers with whom he had gone out
collecting door-to-door on Newark's benighted "colored debit," coming home long after dark with his
clothes smelling sourly of cheap cooking oil. "There

would be colored families," he now told me, "still paying premiums twenty, thirty years after the death of the insured. Three cents a week. That's what we collected." "How come they kept paying?" "They never said anything to the agent. Somebody died and they never mentioned it. The insurance man came round and they paid him." "Amazing," I said, though it was by no means the first time that I was hearing his stories of the eerie evenings collecting pennies from the poorest of Newark's poor, stories from thirty-eight years with the Metropolitan, with Bill and Abe and Sam and J. M. Cohen, all of them, as he reminded me several times, long gone.

And of the few friends alive there wasn't much good news to report, either. "Louie Chesler is in a hospital, pissing blood. Ida Singer is almost blind. Milton Singer can't walk; he's in a wheelchair. Turro —remember Dick Turro?—he has cancer, poor guy. Bill Weber doesn't even know who I am when I call up. 'Herman, Herman who? I don't know any Herman.' He's living with Frankie now but Frankie says they're going to have to put him in a home."

Thus he managed not to dwell entirely on his tumor, speaking instead of the old dead and the dying and those of his friends who would have been better off dead.

The next day I drove to Elizabeth to pick my father up and take him over to University Hospital on Springfield Avenue in Newark; he was to consult

there about an operation with the brain surgeon, Dr.
Meyerson. Lil and he were immediately at logger-
heads when I asked the best way to get to Meyerson's
office. It turned out that Lil was talking about how to
get to Meyerson's office in Millburn, where she had
gone with my father the first time he'd been to see
Meyerson, and he was talking about how to drive to
Meyerson's hospital office, where, unknown to Lil,
this second appointment had been scheduled. In the
car he managed to keep the disagreement simmering
for some time after the confusion had been resolved.

He only quieted down about it when I turned up
from Elizabeth Avenue toward Bergen Street and
began to drive through the most desolate streets of
black Newark. What in my childhood had been the
busy shopping thoroughfares of a lower-middle-
class, mostly Jewish neighborhood were now almost
entirely burned out or boarded up or torn down. The
only ones about seemed to be unemployed black men
—at any rate, black men standing together on the
street corners, seemingly with nothing to do. It was
not a scene conducive to alleviating the gloom of
three people on their way to consult with a brain
surgeon, and yet the rest of the way to the hospital,
my father forgot the encounter awaiting him there
and, instead, reminisced in his random fashion about
who had lived and worked where when he was a boy
before the First World War and on these streets immigrant Jews and their families were doing what they
could to survive and flourish.

"Mr. Tibor lived there. I suppose he was a Hungarian. He made my birthday suit and he made the pants too short. And I couldn't go to my graduation."

"Because the pants were too short?" I asked.

"The suit was useless. That's where Al Schorr's family lived. My God, that's still standing. Remember Al?"

"Sure. How could I forget Al and that voice of his."

"Yeah, well, he had that croaking voice all his life. Rasping like that and deep. Had it when he was a little kid. Al was thrown out of his class. And so he came to my class and I made him treasurer, class treasurer. I was the president. On graduation day we had some money left over, so we went downtown to spend it."

"I see," I said, " 'money left over.' When the guys go into the banks with the masks and the guns that's what they usually say to the teller. They say, 'Excuse me, do you happen to have any money left over?' "

My words managed to lighten up his gloom by about a milliwatt. "Well," my father said, "Al was a great guy. He didn't do it with a gun. He did it with a laugh. He did everything with a laugh. He worked with me until we fired him. I got him in the insurance business. Every job Al ever had I got him. But he was stealing money and he says, 'Hey,' he says, 'hey, they're after me, Herman, the police are after me.' 'Well,' I says, 'here's five dollars, go to the sweat

baths in New York.' And I gave him five dollars and
he went to New York. And he come back, then he
paid the company off and I got him a job with Louie
Chesler. He sold. I told him, if he ever stole from
Louie, I said, I'd shoot him. He worked for the Shu-
berts in Newark. The theater. He used to pick the
tickets, that the people would tear in half, off the
ground. He would put them together, put 'em in a
box, and steal the money. His mother had to pay up,
I don't know, two, three thousand dollars. His
teacher threw him out of his class, that's how we
became friends. He looked around the classroom the
first day in eighth grade—you know what a *pishka*
is," he said to me suddenly, interrupting his story.

"Of course I know. A collection box. Where do
you think I was raised, in Montana?"

"Well, Al looked around the classroom and he
said to his teacher, in that gravel-pit voice, 'If they
paint this room I'll put a dime in the *pishka*.' And *she*
didn't know what *pishka* meant and she threw him
out of the room. And so he came into my room, and
I sized him up, and I made him treasurer. I was
president. Thirteenth Avenue School. God, there it
is, my school."

Meyerson, who David Krohn had assured me was
reputed to be among the best brain surgeons in Jersey, was a plain, plumpish fellow in his early forties,
gentle and extremely amiable right off the bat. When

he had settled in behind his desk, he looked across
to where I was sitting and asked what questions I
had. I pointed to my father, looking awfully glum in
a chair between Lil, whom the doctor had called
"Mrs. Roth," and Meyerson's chief nurse who, we
were told, customarily sat in on preoperative consul-
tations. "My father has the questions," I said. "Go
ahead, Dad. Ask Dr. Meyerson everything you want
to know."

All those questions about the operation that he
had been asking me during the last several days, I
had told him to write down and bring with him for
the consultation. He'd written them in pencil, labo-
riously laid them out in that artlessly sprawling,
yokel handwriting, capitalizing most of the nouns but
spelling all except one or two words correctly. He'd
showed me the list before we left the house and I had
thought, "I want this list. The list and the shaving
mug will do it."

My father removed the piece of lined paper from
his pocket and unfolded it on his lap. "One," he
began. "What's the procedure?" He looked up at
Meyerson. "Pardon my ignorance, Doctor."

Meyerson reached behind him and, from a shelf
with half a dozen medical texts carelessly flopped
over at one end, took down a small painted plastic
model of the brain and the skull. Turning it in his
hand and pointing with a pencil, he explained where
the tumor was situated and where it was pressing
into the brain. He showed us, on the back wall of the

skull, where he could cut through to go in to remove it. "We'll just lift the brain a little here and take out what's growing underneath it."

The thought of his "lifting" my father's brain staggered me. I hadn't believed you could do such a thing to a brain without inviting disaster. And for all I knew, you couldn't.

"What do you use to go in there?" my father asked. "General Electric or Black and Decker?"

He had been looking so ancient and so vanquished that I was surprised by his mordancy and the objective courage it seemed to attest to.

The doctor's reply demonstrated his own quiet objectivity. "Surgical companies make the tools."

My father returned to the next prepared question. "Two. Will it grow back?"

"Eventually it might," Meyerson said. And now it was he who was mildly, mordantly ironic. "Maybe in ten or fifteen years we'll have to do it again."

My father registered the point wryly with a single, slow nod. "Three," he said, returning to his list again. "How much pain is there?"

"No, there isn't much pain," Meyerson told him. "You'll be pretty sick afterward. You'll have a high fever. You'll be very weak."

Meyerson's nurse, a slight, peppy middle-aged woman wearing ordinary street clothes, no less pleasant and genial a person than the doctor, put her hand sympathetically on my father's and said, "We'll try to get you up and sitting five or six days later."

In response, my father simply mumbled, "Oh boy." Five or six days unable to lift himself off the bed gave him the picture, if he hadn't got it already.

He didn't give out, however, but proceeded to his fourth question. "How long does the operation take?"

"Anywhere," Meyerson replied, "from eight to ten hours."

He managed to take that in without flinching, which was better than I did. Eight to ten hours, then five to six days, and what would he be worth after that? After the impoverished childhood and the limited education, after the failure of the shoe store and of the frozen-food business, after the struggle to gain a managerial role in the teeth of the Metropolitan's Jewish quotas, after the premature deaths of so many loved ones—brothers Morris, Charlie, and Milton in the 1920s and '30s, his young niece Jeanette and his young nephew David and his beloved sister-in-law Ethel in the 1940s—after all that he had weathered and survived without bitterness or brokenness or despair, wasn't eight to ten hours of brain surgery really asking too much? Isn't there a limit?

The answer is yes, yes absolutely, yes to the thousandth degree—this *was* asking too much. To "Isn't there a limit?" the answer is no.

"Most of the operating time," Meyerson explained, "is spent getting in through the skull. It depends then on the kind of tumor I find. In that area, ninety-five percent, ninety-eight percent are benign. There isn't much bleeding generally. If there

is—because of the nature of the tumor—that can
slow things up a little."

On he went, the stoical father whom I had never
admired more in his life. "Five. Will I have to learn
to walk again afterward?"

"Yes," Meyerson said. And just when I had
thought that *I* had the picture, I realized that not by
any means had I grasped as yet the awfulness of this
thing. "Yes," Meyerson said, "you probably will."

There were another five questions written down
on the piece of paper but even my father had heard
enough. Pushing the list back into his pocket, he
looked directly at Meyerson and said, "I've got a
problem."

"You do," Meyerson agreed.

This time we drove through the ruins of Newark in
silence. He had nothing more to ask, his childhood
recollections were spent, he did not even have it in
him to improve Lil—there was only that final exchange in Meyerson's office for all of us to think
about and think about. Meyerson had agreed that we
should now solicit a second neurosurgical opinion,
but assuming as he did that the second doctor confirmed his judgment and we decided to go ahead with
surgery at University Hospital, he advised us to have
it sooner rather than later and to set up a tentative
appointment for the operation on the first open date
in his calendar. It turned out to be the anniversary of
my mother's death seven years earlier.

At the apartment Lil went into the kitchenette to prepare some Campbell's soup for lunch. My father went in after her to get the dishes to set the dining room table, and I sat in the living room trying to envision how Meyerson was going to lift my father's brain without damaging it. "There must be ways," I thought.

Lil was apparently using the manual opener screwed to the wall beside the sink, because I heard my father telling her, "Hold the can from the bottom. You're not holding it from the bottom."

"I know how to open a can of soup," she said.

"But you're not holding it right."

"Herman, let me be. I *am* holding it right."

"Why can't you just do what I ask you when I ask you? It *isn't* right. Hold it from the *bottom.*"

And from the other room I had all I could do not to shout, "You're on the brink of a catastrophe, you idiot—let her open the can any fucking way she wants!" though I was also telling myself, "Of course. How to open a soup can. What else is there to think about? What else is there that matters? This is what's kept him going for eighty-six years and what, if anything, is going to get him through now. Hold it from the bottom, Lil—he knows what he's saying."

Admittedly, he went overboard about how she was heating up—or failing to heat up—the soup. After setting our three places at the table, he returned to the kitchenette and stood next to her over the saucepan. She kept insisting the soup wasn't hot yet and he kept insisting it had to be—it didn't take all day to heat up a can of vegetable soup. This exchange was repeated four times, until his patience—if that is the word—ran out and he pulled the pot off the burner and, leaving Lil empty-handed at the stove, came into the dining room and poured the soup into the bowls and onto the place mats and over the table. Maybe because of his bad eyes, he didn't see the extent of the mess he'd made.

The soup was cold. Nobody said so. He probably didn't even notice.

Halfway through the silent meal he said, matter-of-factly, "This is the last chapter," but kept spooning soup into his lopsided mouth until his bowl was empty and his shirt looked as though he had been painting with the soup.

As I was leaving to go back to New York, he went into the bedroom and returned with a small package for me. A couple of brown paper bags had been savagely twisted about to accommodate the contents and then bound together with varying lengths of Scotch tape, most of which were coiled up on themselves like strands of DNA. I spotted the wrapping as his handiwork and I recognized his penmanship as well—with a Magic Marker he had written in uneven block letters across the top fold of the wrapping, "From a Father To a Son."

"Here," he said. "Take this home."

Downstairs in the car I tore off all the wrappings and found my grandfather's shaving mug.

4

I Have to
Start Living Again

From the hotel later that afternoon I phoned Claire in London and my brother in Chicago and recounted what had happened at Meyerson's office, gave them the tentative date for the surgery, and told them about the plan to get a second opinion. But that evening, after having been out alone for a bowl of pasta I couldn't eat and then watching the Mets as though

baseball were a game I couldn't fathom, I found that
I was afraid to try to go to sleep without talking to
someone and being consoled, if only by a presence
at the other end of the line.

I phoned my friend Joanna Clark, who I figured
might still be awake. Joanna was a Pole who had
married an American, come to Princeton to live, succumbed to drink, divorced, collapsed, recovered,
and, probably of all my friends, had endured the
most torment over the course of her life. She could
also be funny about the two of us. "I pollute you with
fumes, I shower you with murky stories, I make foolish jokes in my broken English, and, really, you only
want to have a little Eastern European chat. Well,
nothing comes free. Some Poles are crazykins and I
am one—harmless, I believe." At the very beginning
of the war, in September 1939, her father had been
killed by German artillery. "I don't remember my
father at all," she had told me one evening when I'd
stopped off in Princeton for dinner. I was on my
regular trip up to New York from Philadelphia,
where I was teaching at the University of Pennsyl-
vania. In those years Joanna was usually already
half-drunk when she picked me up in her car at the
Junction train station, and her babble while driving
—about Gombrowicz, Witkiewicz, Schulz, Konwicki
—was alarmingly mythomaniacal, brilliantly eccentric, terrifically informative, and, to me, not unallur-
ing. She was dour and sober-sounding about her
father, however, as we wove back along the road into

Princeton. "He was shot in the trench. Defending Warsaw. In fact, he was carried by his Jewish lieutenant. He was in a trench and he got it. He didn't die right away. He died in the hospital of a wound." "How old was he?" "He was very young. He was thirty-seven." "And so you have no recollection of him." "I was a baby. No, none. Except what I was told."

I looked up her number and dialed at just about the time I used to get her worrying, compulsive phone calls in the old days, back when, even after she'd hid her address book from herself so she wouldn't start phoning people, she fell victim to that mad telephonitis that goes together with drinking and dialed whosever number she could still remember. All I wanted was her ear—having fatherless, courageous, rejuvenated Joanna just listening to me might provide whatever it was *I* now needed at eleven-thirty at night to face putting my own father, at eighty-six, through a ten-hour operation, five lifeless days in bed, three or four months of convalescence, and all of it with no real certainty that it would do him a damn bit of good.

Eighty-six. Eighty-six kept coming in like a knell. I suppose in phoning Joanna I was conceding that even I knew you couldn't have a father forever.

She *was* still awake when I phoned, up waiting for a call from one of her "pigeons"—that's how she referred to the recovering addicts she looked after. At a local recovery program, whose meetings she

attended regularly, she'd become surrogate mother
to some five or six young girls trying to kick drugs.
The girl she was waiting to hear from was moving out
on a deadbeat boyfriend, who the night before, when
she'd told him she was leaving, had bloodied her
nose with one punch.

"Well," I said, "I've been involved in some un-
pleasantness myself. I'm another of your pigeons."

"What is it, Philip?"

"My father is ill."

"Oh, I'm sorry."

"He's facing a very bleak prospect. He has a big
brain tumor. The doctor says it's been growing anywhere from five to ten years. They tell me he's going
to be in desperate shape in a very short time. They're
going to have to try to get it out. It's a terrible operation."

"Does he want it?"

"Want? No. But the alternative is to let it grow
and take the consequences, and that could be gro-
tesque. The problem is that for an eighty-six-year-
old man, even if he survives—and the doctor claims
they survive three times out of four—the recovery
will be a nightmare. He'll never be himself again,
though maybe he can be something close to himself."

"So much closer," Joanna said, "than with that
thing in his head."

"With the thing he's doomed. It's a helluva
choice, but there is no choice."

"With the end of life it always gets that way."

"He's been remarkable. I don't mean in some unusual way, I mean in his own mundane, bull-headed way. His strength amazes me. But what fuels the strength is what makes the situation so awful: the last thing he wants to do is to die."

"It makes you sit and cry," Joanna said.

"Well, I don't cry all the time—mostly I seem to sit in this hotel and do absolutely nothing. Then I think, 'Why am I sitting here when he's over there?' and I drive to Elizabeth and take him for a walk. Tomorrow is going to be the first day that he's really alone. But I don't have it in me to go over again. I need a day off."

"He needs to be alone once in a while, too," she said.

"So there it is," I said. "Anybody's helplessness is difficult, a child's, a friend's, but the helplessness of an old person who once had such vigor . . ."

"Especially of a father."

"Yes. He's fought such a long"—and the adjective that came to me was not one I'd ever thought to associate with his efforts, however much I'd always respected his gumption—"long, long distinguished battle." The word's utter aptness took me by surprise.

"What's good," Joanna said, "is that he has this choice, that he is involved with the choice."

"The choice isn't real, however. The alternative is unacceptable. The choice would be to jump out of the window."

"And you admire that in him, that jumping out of a window for him is an impossible act."

"Admire it and envy it. When I was on the bottom last year, I thought about jumping every day."

"I remember. I had my own stupid times when I thought it was a solution."

"Not him. He doesn't even have it as a fantasy solution. I was over there today to get him to the doctor. I had to drive him across poor, poor, poor old Newark. He knows every street corner. Where buildings are destroyed, he remembers the buildings that were there. You mustn't forget anything—that's the inscription on his coat of arms. To be alive, to him, is to be made of memory—to him if a man's not made of memory, he's made of nothing. 'See those steps, 1917 I was sitting on that stoop with Al Borak—you remember Al Borak? He had the furniture store—I was sitting there with Al the day America went into the war. It was springtime, April or May, I forget. There's where your great-aunt had the candy store. That's where my brother Morris had his first shoe store. Gee, is that still there?' he says. On and on. We passed his school, Thirteenth Avenue School, where he was the teacher's favorite. 'My teacher, she loved me. "Herman," she said—' On he goes all the way across the city."

"Well, life."

"You can say that again. We get to the hospital and he says, 'What a blessing for the city of Newark when they built this hospital.' So he's thinking not about his tumor but about the city of Newark. *He's* the bard of Newark. That really rich Newark stuff isn't my story—it's his."

"He's a good citizen."

"I drive him around, I sit with him, I eat with him, and all the time I'm thinking that the real work, the invisible, huge job that he did all his life, that that whole generation of Jews did, was making themselves American. The *best* citizens. Europe stopped with him."

"Oh, not entirely. He hasn't given up Europe entirely," she said. "The Europe in him is his survivorship. These are people who will never give up. But they are better than Europe, too. There was gratitude in them and idealism. That basic decency."

That was why I'd called Joanna—that was what she shared with my father and what I prized in both of them: survivorship, survivorhood, survivalism.

"Did I ever tell you what happened when he was mugged a couple of years ago? He could have got himself killed."

"No. Tell me."

"A black kid about fourteen approached him with a gun on a side street leading to their little temple. It was the middle of the afternoon. My father had been at the temple office helping them with mailing or something and he was coming home. The black kids prey on the elderly Jews in his neighborhood even in broad daylight. They bicycle in from Newark, he tells me, take their money, laugh, and

go home. 'Get in the bushes,' he tells my father. 'I'm
not getting in any bushes,' my father says. 'You can
have whatever you want, and you don't need that
piece to get it. You can put the piece away.' The kid
lowers the gun and my father gives him his wallet.
'Take all the money,' my father says, 'but if the wallet's of no value to you, I wouldn't mind it back.' The
kid takes the money, gives back the wallet, and he
runs. And you know what my father does? He calls
across the street, 'How much did you get?' And the
kid is obedient—he *counts* it for him. 'Twenty-three
dollars,' the kid says. 'Good,' my father tells him—
'now don't go out and spend it on crap.' "

Joanna laughed. "Well, he's not guilty, your father. Of course he treats him like a son. He knows
that the Jews in Białystok were not responsible for
the New England slave trade."

"It's that—it's more. He doesn't experience
powerlessness in the usual way."

"Yes, he's oblivious to it," she said. "He won't
give in to it. It makes for terrific insensitivity but also
for terrific guts."

"Yes, what goes into survival isn't always
pretty. He got a lot of mileage out of never recogniz-
ing the differences among people. All my life I have
been trying to tell him that people are different one
from the other. My mother understood this in a way
that he didn't. Couldn't. This is what I used to long
for in him, some of her forbearance and tolerance,
this simple recognition that people are different and
that the difference is legitimate. But he couldn't

grasp it. They all had to work the same way, want the same way, be dutiful in the same way, and whoever did it different was *meshugge*—crazy."

"I understand what *meshugge* is, Philip, even if I am a Pole."

"Of course he's not the first person to have such thoughts. But he had his own particular Jewish style of insisting on his absolutely totalistic notions of what is good and what is right, and as a kid it really used to get me down. Everybody has to do it exactly the same way. The way he does it."

"Well, you are relentless, too, you know. It's in you, too, a certain relentlessness that you got from him. You, too, are not always so tactful when you think you are right."

"So Claire tells me."

"You've forgiven him. You've forgiven him that relentlessness and that tactlessness, that wanting to make everybody over in the same mold. All children pay a price, and the forgiveness entails forgiveness also for the price you paid. You talk about him in a very reconciled way."

"I should hope so. Since my mother died, I've got awfully close to him. It would have been easier the other way."

"It wouldn't. The death of a parent, it's horrible. When my mother died," she said, "I had no idea that I would feel that way. Half, or more, of life goes. You feel poorer, you know: somebody who knew me all those years . . ."

"I sat with him and with the neurosurgeon

today, said to be the best in New Jersey, a very kind
fellow about forty, forty-five years old, a puffy, genial
Jewish boy, got good grades, not very athletic—to
look at him, I wouldn't trust him to carve my Thanks-
giving turkey." I told her how the doctor had asked
me if I had any questions and I had told him that my
father had the questions, and how my father had sat
there reading the list of questions, and how the doctor had showed him, on the model of the brain, the
crazy thing he was going to do. "He is going to chop
his head open, pick his brain up, and cut away inside
his skull with a laser, with a beam of light—and I
thought, 'I know where people's weaknesses come
from, we all know that, but where is the source of
the strength? Where does the strength come from in
two men facing this situation this way?' "

"From self-esteem," she said. "They think well
of themselves."

"Is that it? I don't know. I'm sure this is all very
elementary but it's got me stumped tonight. You
don't need surreal art, you know. This is surreal to
me. Those two men sitting there, facing what they
were facing."

"And where is Claire?" Joanna asked.

"In London. At home. She gets upset when I
call. She's said she wants to come back to help but I
told her to stay put and do what she has to do there.
In a way it's actually better alone, moping about by
myself, rather than having her here to drag down,
too. I'd just drive back from Jersey and sit and stare

at her—better to sit and stare by myself. It's better to be concentrated on what has to be done. Though all the concentration isn't so wonderful either. I can't read, God knows I can't write—I can't even watch a stupid baseball game. I absolutely cannot think. I can't do a thing."

"You don't have to. That's also your father," she said, laughing at me now. "You don't have to work all the time."

"It'll be strange and lonely without him. And who understood that?"

"Well, you don't have to understand everything, either."

"I don't understand anything."

I took a shower later, repeating those words. I clipped my toenails, sitting at the edge of the bed—the first thing in days I'd been able to concentrate on other than him—repeating those words. Four words again, very, very basic stuff, but that night, after Joanna had done me the favor of hearing me out, it sounded like all the wisdom in the world to me. I didn't understand anything. As I'd driven back to Manhattan that afternoon with my grandfather's shaving mug clutched in one hand, certainly nothing could have been clearer to me than how little I knew. It wasn't that I hadn't understood that the connection to him was convoluted and deep—what I hadn't known was how deep deep can be.

I slept fitfully till four in the morning, then I turned on the light, got out of bed, and looked at the pictures of his brain again, understanding nothing about that either.

Had it been the MRI of Yorick's brain that Hamlet had been looking at, even he might have been speechless.

A few days later we got the second opinion, and my father preferred it to the first. Vallo Benjamin, a neurosurgeon at NYU Hospital in Manhattan, had agreed to fit us in at the request of David Krohn, who had described him to me as "world-class." Benjamin was an authoritative, worldly man of about my age, a smartly dressed, dark-eyed foreigner, virilely good-looking in the forthright school of Picasso, whom he resembled. He listened to the medical history my father recounted, asked if he got headaches or dizzy spells, then touched the point of a pin to the two sides of my father's face to determine how much feeling he'd lost on the bad side. Benjamin looked to be scrutinizing him very carefully as my father answered all the questions, asked his own questions, and waited to hear if a stay of execution might be granted and his sentence lifted, leaving him free to feel as though he were forty again. "I feel like forty" was something he'd told everyone, even on days when it wasn't true, until just a few months back.

Benjamin stuck the MRI pictures of the brain up on the lighted screen behind his desk and told me to come around and take a look at them with him. My father sat docilely beside Lil, holding in his hand his piece of paper with the list of questions, while the doctor, speaking so softly that only I could hear, traced a finger over the pictures to show me the extensiveness of the tumor. Strictly speaking, he said, it wasn't a brain tumor. Probably it had begun as a tumor on a facial nerve and grown to where now it was not only pushing against the brain stem but extruding through the bone at the back of the nose. Meyerson had estimated that it would take eight to ten hours to operate and had called the operation routine. Now I was told that it would more likely take thirteen or fourteen hours and that the operation involved working where all the arteries and nerves are massed together—"tricky terrain," the doctor said. "Are you telling me it's impossible?" I asked him. "Not at all," he snapped back, as though I had impugned his expertise. "It can be done, of course."

When we sat back down, my father said to Benjamin, "Doctor, I have a friend in the building. His brother-in-law had a tumor like this and they radiated it. Used radiation and it went away. I'm not saying that would solve everything, be permanent. But if I could just have another couple of years . . ."

"Mr. Roth," he replied, very gently, "I don't know if radiation would be effective until I know the kind of tumor we're dealing with. To know that, I need, in addition to these pictures, a CAT scan to give us a picture of the skull as well as the situation with the brain. I then need a biopsy of the tumor.

Yours could be one of three kinds of tumors, and only after a biopsy can I determine which it is and what to suggest to you, sir."

"I see," replied my father glumly.

"The biopsy is done with a needle," the doctor told him. "It's a procedure that takes no more than an hour. I would recommend that you come into the hospital overnight so that we can watch you afterward. You would go home the next day."

"Where do you stick the needle?" my father asked, his tone indicating that nobody was going to torture him without explaining beforehand.

My father's unembellished style and the fight that was obviously still in him despite his age and all he was up against seemed somewhat to beguile the sophisticated neurosurgeon and even to touch some chord of personal sympathy. Several times, in recounting the history of his illness, my father had veered off into an anecdote out of his Newark childhood some seventy-five years earlier, a narrative whose subterranean message appeared to be that he had learned to be realistic on Rutgers Street and was prepared for whatever befell him now. He and life went way, way back together, and he wanted Benjamin to know that too.

To each story—whether about standing up to the Irish ruffians from "down neck" in Newark or working after school in his cousin's blacksmith shop —the doctor listened with nearly as much curiosity as impatience, and he kindly waited to steer him

back to the business at hand until my father had
illustrated his point. Then he explained to him in
detail how the needle would be inserted up through
the roof of the mouth, the tissue removed from the
tumor with the needle, and so on, step by step.

"And radiation?" my father asked again, a little
desperately this time.

"The biopsy will determine if it is the kind of
tumor that responds to radiation. There is always a
chance, though given the size of your tumor and the
length of time you probably have had it, not a great
one."

"Understand," my father said, "I'm talking
about just another three or four years . . ."

The doctor nodded; he understood very well.
The original request for a couple more years had, in
a matter of minutes, been extended to three or four,
I noticed. My father was obviously coming to trust
and even to imbue with a certain divine might this
doctor who was at once so much more patrician and
potent-looking than *haimisher*, heavyset Dr. Meyerson, who had proposed to do rather more than stick
a needle up through the roof of his mouth. It occurred to me that if we were all to sit and talk together in Benjamin's office for another day or two,
my father would eventually overcome his fear of calling down even worse misery upon himself by appear-
ing sinfully greedy and proclaim to this doctor what
had to be in his heart, which was that he wanted not
just three or four years more, but to tackle the whole

damn thing all over again: "I raised myself up out of
the immigrant streets without even a high school education, I never knuckled under, never broke the
law, never lost my courage or said 'I quit.' I was a
faithful husband, a loyal American, a proud Jew, I
gave two wonderful boys every opportunity I myself
never had, and what I am demanding is only what I
deserve—another eighty-six years! Why," he would
ask him, "should a man die at all?" And of course,
he would have been right to ask. It's a good question.

"A needle," my father was saying, "sticking a
needle—is that safe?"

"Generally it's a very safe procedure," the doctor told him. "You'll feel nothing. You will have a
general anesthetic. Afterward, for two or three days,
your mouth will be quite sore but that will go away."

"And then," my father said, "if it's the right
tumor, radiation . . . ?"

The doctor raised his two hands in a sign of
helplessness, looking for the first time not like a
world-class neurosurgeon but a bargaining businessman in an Oriental bazaar. "It's not wholly impossible and I can't rule it out entirely, but right now I
don't know."

"What are the effects of radiation?" my father
asked.

"If you were a young person, you might be affected about thirty years later."

"But one thing is certain, if I understand correctly—you don't want to operate."

"I wouldn't and I couldn't. I have to know first exactly what I'd find inside."

When we left the doctor's office, I suggested that instead of his going directly home, we take the elevator downstairs to the hospital cafeteria and, while the consultation was fresh in our minds, go over what the doctor had said.

We found a table for four—with us also was my nephew Seth, who lives in Jersey City with his wife and who had driven Lil and my father from Elizabeth and was going to drive them back. Seth had sat out in the waiting room during the consultation, and partly for his information but mainly to be sure that my father hadn't misunderstood, in the cafeteria I went over everything again, emphasizing that though the doctor had left open the possibility of the tumor being susceptible to treatment by radiation, that wasn't the likely eventuality.

"I like this man," my father said when I had finished. "I'm impressed by this man. The other guy just wanted to go in and cut. This man wants all the information first. I'm impressed by him. Weren't you?" he asked Lil. "Impressed by him?"

"Yes," Lil said. "He seemed very nice."

"Were you, Phil?"

"Yes. I'm sure he's an excellent doctor. David assured me he was."

"That's right. And he said wait. What is he?" my father asked me. "A Jew?"

"I believe so. I think a Persian Jew."

"Good-looking man," my father said.

There were crowds outside the elevator on the main floor, and pushing through the busy hospital lobby, I held him by one arm while Seth took the other. "I have to start living again," my father suddenly told me. "I can't hole up in that apartment anymore. I can't be a hermit."

"Absolutely," I said.

"I have to go back to the Y. The cantor from the synagogue came to see me—did I tell you? Two men from the synagogue and the cantor. They'd heard about the tumor. They said they'll drive me every day to the Y."

"Good. Go."

"I didn't know I had so many friends," he said.

"A reprieve," I thought, "and let him enjoy it. Enjoy it yourself," I thought, "if only till the next decision has to be made tomorrow." And so that night I managed to watch the Mets game with some pleasure, concentrating, like any ordinary run-of-the-mill escapist, on Darling's three-hitter and McReynolds's home run rather than on my father and the tumor that was still there inside his head despite the Mets' victory, blindly, massively there, and that, if left there, would in the end be as merciless as a blind mass of anything on the march.

Two years earlier, on October 14, 1986, I unfortunately had to be in London while the Mets were play-

ing Houston in game five of the play-offs. It was
eleven-fifteen London time when I phoned him in
Elizabeth, and my father was ecstatic. I'd got him to
take an interest in the Mets only that spring, when
he was laid low for about a month by a debilitating
malaise that nobody could diagnose and that probably had had something to do with the brain tumor.
His strength deserted him almost completely, he had
no appetite for food, and sometimes when he got up
to walk he listed from side to side. I'd flown back
from London to find out what was wrong, and during
the weeks I'd stayed on in New York, I had tried to
divert his attention from this unexplained illness by
getting him interested in the Mets, who were on the
way to winning the pennant. I would come over some
evenings for dinner and watch the game with him,
and when I went out to a couple of games at Shea
Stadium, I'd told him to keep his eyes open and see
if he could spot me in the stands. By the time I left
his symptoms had all but disappeared and he was
nearly fit again, and also very much a fan—and a fan
for the first time, really, since I was a small boy and
he used to take my brother and me out to Ruppert
Stadium in Newark to see the old Triple-A Newark
Bears play a Sunday doubleheader against our rivals
from across the marshes, the Jersey City Giants.

When I wound up in London during the play-
offs, I phoned him each night to find out about the
games. I loved his exuberant descriptions.

"Mets won," he told me as though it had been a

triumph for him as well. "Twelfth inning. A helluva game. Gooden against Ryan. Strawberry hit a home run. Then they tied it. *Helluva* game."

"Whoa. Slow down," I said. "When did Strawberry hit the home run?"

"In the sixth. They won in the twelfth. Backman hits a ball too hot for the third baseman. Couldn't hold on to it. He got on first. Then the pitcher for the Houston Astronauts threw a wild pitch to first and he went to second. So there was no sense pitching to Hernandez and he put him on. Then Carter came up. He is 0 for twenty-two or twenty-three. And he hit the ball back up the middle, Backman scored, and that was it. Mets won two to one."

"Great. How long ago did it end?" I asked.

"About half an hour ago. Hey, did you hear about your friend Wiesel?"

"Yeah, somebody told me about it." The novelist Elie Wiesel, whom I had known slightly years ago, had won the Nobel Peace Prize that day.

"A hundred and twenty thousand bucks, plus the honor," my father said. "So this year he's the third Jew to win one."

"Is that right? Who are the other two?"

"This guy Cohen and this Italian-Jewish girl named Levysomething."

"Well," I said, "it's a great day for the Jews and a great day for the Mets. Mets two, Houston one— Jews three, Gentiles nothing. Now they're going down to Houston, right? And play tomorrow?"

"Right. They just have to win one," he said.

"Well," I said, "stranger things have happened than losing two in a row."

"No," he said, "they can't drop two, they're too good. Today was a *helluva* game."

"If it goes to seven they'll have to face Scott again," I said.

"Phil, they'll beat him. First of all, he's pitching for the second time after three days' rest. Or is it four days' rest? There was the rain-out, then today, Wednesday—it'll be three days' rest."

"Okay," I said, "you say they'll beat him, I believe you. I'll speak to you tomorrow. And congratulations on Wiesel. You Jews ought to be proud."

"Ah, cut that crap out, will ya?" he said, but he was laughing when he hung up.

And laughing when I called the next night. "Well, what happened?" I said.

"It's still on. You wouldn't believe it. Thirteenth inning."

"My God."

"They were behind three one in the ninth but it's now the thirteenth inning and it's tied score. I'm watching it now. I didn't even eat."

"One game's closer than the other," I said.

"It's beautiful," he said.

"Well, I'm going to sleep," I said. "It's eleven-thirty here. I figured it would be over by now because they started at three."

"No. It's two out in the top of the thirteenth inning."

"Who's pitching for the Mets?"

"McDowell is pitching and Anderson is pitching for the Houstons."

"Well, I'm going to have to go to sleep," I said.

But at midnight, after having brushed my teeth and gone to bed, I got out of bed and came down to the kitchen to call him again. I wasn't just calling because of the Mets. "What happened?" I asked him.

"Phil? Oh, my God, it's *unbelievable*."

"Still playing?"

"The Mets went ahead four three just after you hung up. Strawberry—and I think Dykstra got him around. And then this guy hit a home run in the Houston bottom of the fourteenth. And now it's the top of the fifteenth. It's four four and there's some fat Mexican pitching."

"Oh, yeah, that very attractive fellow."

"The Mets have got this very young shortstop up, who can only strike out. . . . No—pop-up. He popped up. Well, that isn't a strikeout. Hey, I'm giving you this pitch by pitch to London, it's going to cost you a fortune."

But pitch by pitch I was enjoying it enormously, maybe even more than if I had been there. "Go ahead, Herm. I'm a rich man. Pitch by pitch. Who's up?"

"They got Hernandez and Carter coming up. It's been an unbelievable game, but it was three nothing going into the ninth. The Mets had only got two hits. You know something? It's almost time for the Red

Sox to get started. That's supposed to start at eight
o'clock and here it is seven already. Upps, Keith
struck out."

"He struck out? This game's going to go on all
night."

He laughed loudly. "I think so."

"Okay. I'll give you a ring tomorrow to see what
happened. Here's hopin'."

"Don't you worry, they'll win. You just get some
sleep," he said.

At seven the next morning his time—noon London time—he phoned to tell me the results.

"Phil?"

"Yes."

"It's Dad. You've never seen anything like it.
Mets won in the sixteenth."

"Great. I was going to phone you a little later."

"I only just got up. I knew you'd be wondering.
They were down three in the ninth. Did I tell you this
last night, about the ninth?"

"Don't worry. Tell me everything."

"Get this. They get three runs in the ninth. They
go ahead four three. That pitcher is in there."

"Kerfeld, for Houston?"

"No. For the Mets. I can never think of his
name."

"McDowell."

"No. The other guy."

"Orosco."

"Yeah, Morosco. The Mets go ahead four three.

Then Houston gets a home run, ties it up four four. In the sixteenth inning the Mets get three runs. They go ahead seven four. Houston gets up. Guy gets on base and the next guy gets a home run. Seven six. And then Kevin Bass strikes out and they won the game seven six."

"So they won the series."

"They won the series."

"How'd the Mets get the three runs?"

"Dykstra. I'm telling you! After Morosco gave up the runs in the sixteenth, Hernandez came out to the mound—I just read this in the paper—and you know what he said to him? 'If you throw another fastball, I'll kill you.' "

"I wonder if he would have."

"*I* would have," my father said, laughing, and sounding as though whatever had floored him in the spring was a fluke and he was going to live a thousand years.

Our reprieve lasted about twenty-four hours. Then the brain tumor took charge again.

For the next month and a half nothing happened and nothing was done—none of us knew what exactly *to* do. Since the first neurosurgeon had said that the tumor would not respond to radiation and the second had indicated that the chances radiation would help were small, the biopsy began to seem an ordeal that we had no business forcing on him, par-

ticularly as I had learned by asking around that it
could be very painful and, given where the needle
was to be blindly inserted, not without some risk.
And if the result was only to present us with the
option we already dreaded—an operation that could
leave him worse off rather than better—what was
gained by subjecting him to it?

To make things more difficult, only a few days
after our consultation Dr. Benjamin left America for
over a month to lecture in Europe, and there was no
way that I could air my doubts with him until his
return on June 20. He had given us the name of
someone to whom he was willing to entrust the biopsy, but though my father went back over to New
York to see that doctor—this time accompanied by
my brother, who had flown in from Chicago for a
week to be with him and to spell me a little—we all
felt there were too many unanswered questions to
proceed before Dr. Benjamin's return, if at all.

And my father was hardly equipped to make the
decision to go ahead on his own. He'd conducted
himself gallantly with the two brain surgeons, but
now, caught in the vise of their differing proposals,
he succumbed to a wild helplessness. He began to
say things to me that didn't make much sense, and
then for longer periods said nothing or suddenly, un-
provoked, lashed out at Lil so uncontrollably that
even he was startled afterward by his vehemence and
meekly apologized. Apologizing to Lil would not have
seemed like an unfortunate development had it not

signaled demoralization rather than remorse. He repeated to me, to my brother, to everyone, that he
didn't want a biopsy or an operation through the back
of his head or the roof of his mouth—all he wanted
was what he had wanted from the start: to be able to
see his food and to read his paper and, as he put it,
to "navigate" on his own. Why couldn't they just
remove the cataract from his good eye and give him
back his sight? I found a draft of a letter to the
ophthalmologist on the dining room table one day
when I came over for lunch: "Dear Dr. Krohn, I want
my sight back. I want my eye fixed. That's what I
want. Herman Roth"

Of course, as the days passed and he dangled
impotently in despair, I could not forget that Dr.
Meyerson, who had never struck me as a fool, had
warned us that things were going to get worse "in a
relatively short time" unless something was done.
Meyerson had told us that to remove the tumor he
would go in through the back of the skull and take
eight to ten hours to get it out, and Benjamin had told
us that to remove the tumor he would go up through
an incision in the roof of the mouth—following something like the route of the biopsy needle—and extract
it in thirteen or fourteen hours, and my father was
telling me that the one prospect was as horrifying as
the other and that submitting to either was unthinkable. "All I want is my sight back. I want to see!"

In bed I'd think, "Listen to him. Listen to what
he is saying. He is telling you what he wants and it's

very simple. He wants his eye fixed. He's not a child
—he's made it through eighty-six years on his own
kind of wisdom, so honor that wisdom and just give
him what it is he wants." But then, in the next minute, it would seem to me that by yielding to his un-
realistic appraisal of the crisis I was only trying to
evade the hard choice . . . and so around again I
went, unconvinced that there was any reward com-
mensurate with the risks involved in surgery, yet
conscious that if nothing was done, *in a relatively
short time* his condition could deteriorate horribly.

One morning, after my brother had flown back
to Chicago, I made a call to Palm Beach, to Sandy
Kuvin, a doctor cousin of ours. Over the years, at my
request, he had been checking in on my father when
my father was vacationing in Florida, and he had
given us sensible advice about such health problems
as had cropped up for my father down there. Sandy
was a couple of years older than I, a father of three
college kids and a vigorous supporter of Israel, who
spent nearly half his working year at a medical research clinic in Jerusalem for which he'd raised the
endowment and which was named for him. I'd made
a tour of the place with one of his staff the last time
I'd been in Jerusalem. We'd all grown up in the same
part of Newark, we'd gone to the same high school
in the forties, and though he and I had only met up
again recently—when I began visiting my father in
Florida each winter—our annual evening together at
a local restaurant and our afternoons at his airy

house on a Palm Beach inlet had been friendly and enjoyable, each of us getting a kick out of seeing how far the other fellow had traveled from the halls of Weequahic High.

After I explained the situation and described to him my indecision, Sandy said to me, "He's an old man, Philip—he's lived a long life and by now that tumor is growing pretty slowly. In ten years or so it's caused no more damage than the hearing loss in one ear and the facial paralysis on one side of his face. Maybe some of his headaches come from it, and it may be that when he walks some of his uncertainty isn't just from the bad vision but from this thing pressing on the eighth nerve. But the damage hasn't been ruinous and it may never be."

"But the damage you speak of has all happened in the last six months. What's going to happen in the next six months?"

"Nobody knows. Maybe nothing," he said, "and maybe everything. If he wants his vision, give him his vision, and if he has it for as little as a month before he dies, well, he will at least have had what he wanted for a month. Maybe he'll be lucky and have it for longer."

"That's what I've been thinking—when I'm not thinking the opposite. Doc, will you do me a favor? Will you telephone him? Don't let on that we spoke. Call him out of the blue and let him tell you his story and then tell him what you told me—that it's growing slowly and to forget it. Because he's really headed

for the bottom if something doesn't lift him soon. He
might just keel over and call it quits out of sheer
emotional agony."

Within half an hour my father phoned me,
sounding vigorous and full of bounce, as though
wholly reempowered. Chinning himself up on life
again.

"Guess who just invited me to his daughter's
wedding in December?"

"Who?"

"Sandy Kuvin called from Palm Beach. You
know what he said? I told him what's happening and
he said, 'Herman, forget it. You've had it for ten
years and the pace that it's growing at is so slow that
you can have it for another ten years before it does
any more harm.' Kuvin told me I could be killed by
ten other things before the tumor gets any larger."
With something that sounded like real delight, he
enumerated for me the potential killers. "I could get
a heart attack, I could get a stroke, I could get cancer
—before that thing kills me, a hundred other things
could finish me off."

I had to laugh. "Well, that's great news."

"Kuvin says forget it and get on with my life."

"Did he? Then maybe that's what you ought to
do."

"His Michelle, his daughter, is getting married
on—here, I wrote it down—on Tuesday, December
27, 1988. At their house. Eleven-thirty a.m. He wants
you to come to the wedding, too. With me and Lil."

December was seven months off. Did that or did that not constitute "a relatively short time"? "If you go, I'll go," I said.

"Phil, I want my eyesight back. I want Dr. Krohn to fix my eye. Enough farting around with this other thing."

5

Maybe Ingrid
Can Look After Me for Good

But a week after Benjamin returned from Europe, my father went in for the biopsy, not as a prelude to surgery—by that time we were all firmly decided against surgery—but on the possibility, however slight, that the biopsy would disclose a type of tumor that radiation could shrink. I didn't see how, in good conscience, we could simply ignore the tumor until

we were sure there was nothing to treat it other than
the butchery that was unacceptable to all of us. I
dreaded the thought that the needle that was to be
stuck up through the roof of his mouth could damage
something inside his skull, but I allowed myself to be
convinced by Benjamin that Dr. Persky, who would
perform the procedure, was as skilled a practitioner
as we could find.

The super of his building drove my father and
Lil over to Manhattan to the hospital, where I met
them and, after an interminable bureaucratic delay,
got him registered and up to his room. There he was
given some supper; to my surprise, he was able to
absorb himself completely in the meal. Then Lil left,
and I took him down to be interviewed by a young
resident to whom he told the history of his illness as
well as several brief anecdotes out of his childhood.
Back in his room we got the pajamas out of his overnight case, and after he had been to the bathroom I
helped him into the bed. He was exhausted, and his
face, with the patch off the blind eye on the drooping
side, looked dreadful. Yet he seemed, if anything,
less dejected than he'd been during the period when
nothing was being done. There was a new ordeal to
face, and facing ordeals did not allow for hopeless-
ness. It called forth instead that amalgam of defiance
and resignation with which he had learned to con-
front the humiliations of old age.

At the registration desk downstairs, he had been
told that it cost $3.50 a day to watch the TV set in

the room and he had refused to pay it. When I saw him on the bed staring at the ceiling with the one working eye, I told him that I would pay for it. "Come on," I said. "I'm a sport—I'll blow you to a night's television."

"Three and a half dollars for television? They're out of their minds."

"We can watch the ball game. The Mets are playing the Reds."

"Not for three fifty," he replied adamantly. "The hell with it."

"It beats lying on your bed like that, worrying about tomorrow."

"I'm not worrying. I don't allow myself the luxury. You go home."

"It's only seven. You can watch *MacNeil/Lehrer*."

"Don't worry about me. I'm fine. You get something to eat and go home to the hotel and watch the Mets."

In the chair beside his bed I began to read the late edition of the *Post*. "You want me to read you the news?" I asked.

"No."

"We should have thought to bring a radio. You could have listened to the game on the radio."

"I don't need a radio."

Fifteen minutes later he had fallen asleep and within an hour it looked as though he might well be out for the night, and this before the nurse had even given him the sleeping pill that I had asked the resident to order for him. His teeth were lying on the bedside table where he'd left them. I put them into the plastic dish the hospital provided for dentures and, capping it, put the dish away in the table drawer. These teeth were new ones, made for the lower right side of his mouth. Because of the facial disfigurement, the dentist was having a lot of trouble fitting them precisely; only two days earlier, out taking a walk with me, my father had yanked them from his mouth—"These goddamn things! Too many teeth!"—but then when he had them in his hand he didn't know what to do with them. We were crossing North Broad Street at the time and the light was about to turn against us. "Here," I'd said, "give them to me," and I took the dentures and stuck them in my pocket. To my astonishment, having them in my own hand was utterly satisfying. Far from feeling squeamish or repelled, as I continued along, guiding him by one arm up onto the curb, I was amused by the rightness of it, as though we'd now officially become partners in a comical duo—as though I'd assumed the role of straight man to a clown whose ill-fitting false teeth invariably brought the house down, a joke on a par with Durante's nose or Eddie Cantor's eyes. By taking the dentures, slimy saliva and all, and dumping them in my pocket, I had, quite inadvertently, stepped across the divide of physical estrangement that, not so unnaturally, had opened up between us once I'd stopped being a boy.

I waited beside the bed for another few minutes, and then, as he still gave no sign of awakening, I quietly left him. At the nurse's desk I stopped to find out when he was due to go down to the operating room the next day. Then from a telephone booth at the end of the corridor I phoned my brother in Chicago.

"I hope we're not doing this just to be doing something," I said. "I get that feeling, ever so slightly."

"How is he?"

"Well, this, like everything, he's going to meet head-on. Won't put up with any distraction. They charge three and a half bucks to watch the TV in the room and he told the poor overworked bastard down at the registration office that it was highway robbery."

My brother laughed. "He is a stubborn prick, all right."

"Yeah, well, in the circumstances it may not turn out to be such a bad thing to be a stubborn prick. I'll speak to you tomorrow when he comes up from the operating room. He goes down around noon."

"First Avenue and Thirtieth Street," I told the driver the next day. "University Hospital."

"Good-looking broad you came out of that hotel with," the driver said as we started crosstown. Just before hailing the cab, I'd been talking under the hotel canopy to the wife of an old friend, whom I'd run into as I was leaving the Essex House on the way downtown to the hospital.

"Yes?"

"You jump her bones?" he asked me.

"Pardon?"

"You fuck her?"

In the rearview mirror I saw a pair of green eyes whose truculent glare was even more startling than the question. If I hadn't already lost time talking out in front of the hotel, I would have decided against entrusting my life to those eyes and got out of the cab, but as I wanted to be sure to be at the hospital to see my father before he went in to the operating room, I said, "As a matter of fact, no. One of my friends does. She's his wife."

"What difference does that make? He'd fuck your wife."

"No, this particular friend wouldn't, though I understand it happens." I understood because I'd done it myself on a few occasions but, unlike the driver, I wasn't putting all my cards on the table right off. We had a ways to go yet.

"It happens all the time, buddy," he told me.

I didn't think cutting him was a good idea, so I replied, lightly enough, "Well, it's good to talk to a realist."

He answered me with undisguised contempt. "Is that what they call it?"

Registering for the first time the buildings out

the window, I realized that he had turned in the wrong direction on Park and was driving uptown. "Hey!" I said and reminded him where we were going.

To correct his error he decided to proceed all the way east to the F.D.R. Drive and then "shoot" south. This entailed going even farther in the wrong direction to get onto the drive.

I'd allowed myself far more time than was necessary to get to the hospital by eleven-thirty, but now, because of a tie-up at the entrance to the drive, it was already after eleven before the taxi had even begun to edge toward the heavy flow of southbound traffic.

"You a doctor?" he asked, fixing me, I saw in the mirror, with that warlike look.

"Yes," I said.

"What kind?"

"Take a guess."

"Head," he said.

"That's right."

"Psychiatrist," he said.

"That's right."

"At University Hospital."

"No, up in Connecticut."

"You head of the clinic?"

"Do I look like the head of the clinic?"

"Yeah," he said authoritatively.

"No," I said, "just one of the staff doctors. I'm content with that."

"You're smart—you don't go chasing the buck."

I found myself studying him as though I were
indeed a professional whose interest exceeded that
of an ordinary, transient passenger's. The man was
a mastodon, and though the taxi was a full-size
sedan, he overflowed his half of the front seat and
rose to a fraction of an inch of the ceiling—and in his
hands the wheel was a tiny infant, an infant he was
throttling. Of his face all I could see in the mirror
were those eyes, which looked as though, when they
jumped out of his head, they'd be as capable as his
hands of ending your life. His aura was even more
menacing than his opening remark had suggested,
and I didn't like the idea of "shooting" down the
drive with him, especially since it was clear—and
not only from his having turned the wrong way almost
right off—that his attention was targeted on something more compelling than taking me where I
wanted to go.

"You know something, Doc," he said, swinging
suddenly, with no lack of daring, into the fast lane
going south, "my old man's in his grave now without
his four front teeth. I knocked 'em out of his fucking
mouth for him."

"You didn't like him."

"He was a shit-heel and a failure and he wanted
me to fail, too. Misery loves company. He used to get
my older brother to beat me up on the street. My
older brother beat me up and my old man never
stopped him. So one day when I was twenty I went
up to him and knocked his fucking teeth out and I

said, 'You know what that's for? For never protecting me against Bobby.' I didn't go to his funeral even. But a lot of children don't go to their parents' funeral, do they?" In a voice all at once hollowly, defensively hangdog, he added, "I'm not the first."

In the mirror the eyes that hid nothing brutal or bellicose were waiting on my response.

"You're not the first," I assured him.

"My mother is no better," he said, and "mother" he expectorated, as though it were not a word but something putrid that he'd bit into. "She called me up crying that he was dead and I said, 'Yeah, go ahead, cry for the great hero.' And I told her what a stupid bastard she was."

"You had a rough time of it, didn't you?"

The purity of the paranoia that flared up in those eyes made me think, *light bouncing off the blade of a knife*. But he had me wrong if he believed I was an ironist of the sort who, like his father, needed to go to his grave minus four front teeth. I was a psychiatrist, I did not stoop to judgments, and that, fortunately, seemed to sink in soon enough. He was by no means stupid but, boy, was he lacking in trust. By having failed to protect him from Bobby, his late father had unleashed upon the world one very skeptical younger son.

"Yeah," he replied in a sad voice, "you can call it rough." But butting the air with his head, he added angrily, "I survived."

"You sure have."

Then he astonished me. I would have been no
more surprised had he raised a teacup from the seat
beside him and, with his pinky pointing politely,
daintily taken a little sip. "Doc, I'm insecure."

"You?" Incredulous, I let him have it. "What
the hell are you talking about? You knocked your
father's teeth down his throat, you told your mother
off when she was in tears—this is your cab you're
driving, isn't it?"

"Yeah. I got two."

"*Two*—why, you're as secure as they come."

"Am I?" this violent bastard asked me.

"Seems so to me."

"You're good to me, Doc—I'm taking a buck off
the fare. You shouldn't have to pay for my mistake."
Swinging from the drive onto Thirty-fourth Street, he
grew still more magnanimous. "I'm turning the
meter off right now and taking another buck off the
top."

"If you like. That's very kind of you."

I wondered if I hadn't overdone it. I looked in
the mirror expecting to find that he was ready to kill
me for calling him kind. But no, he *liked* it. This guy
is human, I thought, in the worst sense of the word.

In front of the hospital, when I hopped out of
the cab, I was a good psychiatrist and gave him the
only advice I thought he could actually follow. "Keep
punchin'," I told him.

"Hey, you too, Doc," he said, and the face,
which I now saw was that of a man-baby, of an over-

fleshed, hard-drinking, rancorous infant age forty,
had dissolved into a surfeited smile, indicating that,
on just my first professional outing, a positive trans-
ference had been effected. He actually did it, I realized, annihilated the father. He is of the primal horde
of sons who, as Freud liked to surmise, have it in
them to nullify the father by force—who hate and
fear him and, after overcoming him, honor him by
devouring him. And I'm from the horde that can't
throw a punch. We aren't like that and we can't do
it, to our fathers or to anyone else. We're the sons
appalled by violence, with no capacity for inflicting
physical pain, useless at beating and clubbing, unfit
to pulverize even the most deserving enemy, though
not necessarily without turbulence, temper, even fe-
rocity. We have teeth as the cannibals do, but they
are there, imbedded in our jaws, the better to help
us articulate. When we lay waste, when we efface, it
isn't with raging fists or ruthless schemes or insane
sprawling violence but with our words, our brains,
with mentality, with all the stuff that produced the
poignant abyss between our fathers and us and that
they themselves broke their backs to give us. En-
couraging us to be so smart and such *yeshiva buch-
ers*, they little knew how they were equipping us to
leave them isolated and uncomprehending in the face
of all our forceful babble.

I suppose it was the fear of this drastic outdis-
tancing of my father that had caused me, in my first
years of college, to feel as though I were something

like his double or his medium, emotionally to imagine
that I was there at college in his behalf and that it
wasn't just I who was being educated but he whom I
was delivering from ignorance as well. Just the opposite was happening, of course: every book I under-
lined and marginally notated, every course I took and
paper I wrote was expanding the mental divide that
had been growing wider and wider between us since
I had prematurely entered high school at twelve, just
about the age when he had left school for good to
help support his immigrant parents and all their children. Yet for many months there was nothing my
reasonable self could do to shake off the sense of
merging with him that overcame me in the library
and in the classroom and at my dormitory desk, the
impassioned, if crazy, conviction that I was somehow
inhabited by him and quickening his intellect right
along with mine.

When I reached my father's hospital room, it was
empty. There was nothing of his on the bedside
table, and in the closet I saw that his clothes, his
robe, and his little suitcase were gone. Most frightening to see was the bare mattress, stripped of all its
bedding. I rushed back down the hall to the nurse's
desk, thinking, *"It's over, it's over, he's been spared
the worst,"* and there, to my enormous relief, I
learned that he had simply been taken to the operating room a few minutes earlier. I'd missed him because of the extended session with my own patient,

the parricidal driver. He was not dead. *"But if they stick the needle in the wrong place, if they blind him, if they paralyze the rest of his face . . ."*

It was nearly five when they brought him down from the recovery room and into a room for four post-operative cases, where he was hooked up to the monitoring machines and where a nurse was on duty round the clock. I sat beside his bed until visiting hours were over, watching with wonder as his pulse maintained itself at a steady rate of sixty beats a minute. Around the room the other patients fresh from surgery were registering drastically fluctuating blood pressure readings while his remained virtually fixed at 155 over 78. I couldn't, of course, interpret the EKG pattern flickering steadily across the screen, but it didn't seem to me to be signaling anything erratic or arrhythmical. He was still, systemically, a marvel and therefore fated to be spared nothing.

They had given him ice to suck on to ease the pain inside his mouth. I kept feeding it to him and replenishing the bowl. His mouth hurt so much he could hardly talk. And when he finally had something to say, he made it short and sweet.

"How do you feel now?" I asked after he'd been up from the recovery room for about an hour.

The voice was weak, the tone grim, the message unambiguous. "I wish I were dead."

He did not complain again.

In the bed across the way there was a very frail old Oriental man with a tube inserted directly into his throat. He'd had intestinal surgery and kept gag-ging wretchedly and trying to hawk up phlegm. His daughter, a rather pretty little woman of about forty, terrifically efficient and concentrated entirely on her father, silently went about doing what she could to make him comfortable, but it did not seem possible to alleviate his misery. Though his face remained expressionless, every few minutes we heard him struggling with the tube as if he were about to choke to death.

When I got to the hospital the next morning, I said to my father, "How did you sleep?"

"No good. The Chinaman kept everybody up."

In a chair beside his bed the old man, sitting now, was struggling with the tube, and his daughter was already there silently ministering to him.

"The mouth?" I asked.

He shook his head to indicate that his mouth still felt awful.

The nurse said that the doctor had decided that my father was in too much distress to leave that day. He also hadn't urinated and they couldn't let him go home until he had. My father told me that he hadn't moved his bowels either, and he kept getting out of the bed to go to the toilet and try. Each time I would guide him to the bathroom and then stand outside the door, waiting there in case he needed help. From time to time, the Oriental woman and I looked at each other tending our fathers and smiled.

Lil came to visit; Seth came with his wife, Ruth;

Sandy and Helen phoned him from Chicago; Claire, who was back from London, phoned him from Connecticut; Jonathan phoned him from where he was working out on the road; and then, late in the day, while I was helping him to eat what he could of his watery, unappetizing supper, Dr. Benjamin appeared, tailored splendidly and radiating all the self-assurance that one would hope to see in one's neurosurgeon. He was accompanied by a crisp-looking administrative aide in a tie and a white shirt, who exercised his duty with military precision. By comparison, my father, slumped in front of his supper tray, his food-stained hospital gown ineptly tied at the back, his teeth out and half his face down the drain, looked like a small old lady—and the small old lady he looked like was his mother, Bertha Zahnstecher Roth, as I remembered her in the hospital near the end of her life. I recalled very clearly being home from college and standing beside her bed while *he* was feeding *her* and she was mumbling to him in Yiddish.

Benjamin gave us the results of the biopsy. The tumor was an extremely rare type formed out of a kind of cartilaginous material, "a little like your fingernail," he told my father. It was benign but not susceptible to radiation. He proposed to remove it surgically in two operations, each about seven or eight hours long. The first time he would go in through the mouth to extract part of the bulk that way and then, some months later,

he would go in through the back of the head to extract the rest.

Probably it hadn't been tactically possible for
him, but I wished that the doctor could have taken
me aside to apprise me of all this first. It was a lot to
tell an old man whose strength, that evening, you
could have measured in teaspoons. After the doctor
had spoken his piece, my father looked for a long
time at the tray on which they'd served him another
dinner of cold consommé and yogurt and a chocolate
drink and Jell-O and a Popsicle. It was impossible to
guess from his lost, unfocused gaze what, if anything, he was thinking about. I was thinking of the
fingernail that had been aggrandizing the hollows of
his skull for a decade, the material as obdurate and
gristly as he was, that had cracked open the bone
behind his nose and, with a stubborn, unrelenting
force just like his, had pushed tusklike through into
the cavities of his face.

When finally my father seemed to remember
Benjamin's presence, he looked up and said to him,
"Well, Doctor, I've got a lot of people waiting for me
on the other side," and with his head jutting out
toward the bowl, he dropped his spoon into the Jell-
O and resumed the attempt to eat something.

I walked out into the corridor with the doctor
and his aide. "I don't see how he could survive two
operations like that," I said.

"Your father is a strong man," the doctor replied.

"A strong eighty-six-year-old man. Maybe enough is enough."

"The tumor is at a critical point. You can expect him to have serious trouble within a year."

"With what?"

"Probably with swallowing," he said, and that, of course, evoked a horrible picture, but not much worse than envisioning him recovering not from one eight-hour operation on his head but now from two. The doctor said, "Anything can happen, really."

"We'll have to think it all through," I said.

We shook hands, but as he and his aide started away, he turned back to offer a gentle reminder. "Mr. Roth, once something happens, it may be too late to help him."

"Maybe it's already too late," I replied.

By the next morning he still hadn't urinated, and as he didn't look forward to being catheterized any more than anyone else does, I told him to go into the toilet and turn the water on in the sink and sit there until something happened. He went in three times, and the last time, after twenty minutes, he came out and said it had worked. He made it work.

After I had helped him get into his street clothes, I went off to phone my brother and tell him we were about to check out of the hospital and drive up to the Connecticut house, where Claire and I had moved for the summer. "Well, now we know for sure that there's nothing to do," I said to my brother.

"Two operations are out of the question. You should see what he looks like just from this."

As I packed my father's suitcase with his shaving things, the old man across the way was still choking on the tube in his throat and the daughter was still silently moving about trying to make him comfortable. I went up to say goodbye to her.

"Your father better?" she asked, her English heavily accented and hard to make out.

"For now," I replied.

"Your father is a brave man," she said.

"So is yours," I said. "Old age is no picnic, is it?"

She smiled and shook my hand, probably having failed to understand what I said.

Outside the hospital, as I was leading him very slowly across the parking lot to my car, he said to me, rather like a child who'd been promised a reward for taking some terrible medicine, *"Now* can I have my eye fixed?"

He was to stay in an upstairs bedroom where the windows looked out on the apple trees and the ash trees and the maples. The room had a wood-burning stove in it and a bright-colored North African rug, and it was a room he said that he always loved to sleep in during the years when he'd come to visit with my mother and later, after her death, when he and Lil came up a couple of times each summer for a

weekend with us in the country. I got him upstairs to
take a nap after lunch. That morning Claire had
made a big pot of vegetable soup for him for the next
few days and had cut some flowers in the garden to
liven up his room, but it turned out that he still
couldn't take anything warm in his mouth and was so
worn out from the two-hour drive up from the hospital that he'd just sat staring into the soup bowl, unable to respond to her attempts to make him feel at
home.

In his room he immediately fell asleep on top of
the bedspread; however, when I came to check on
him about twenty minutes later, I saw, as I passed
the partially open door of the bathroom next to his
bedroom, that he was sitting on the toilet holding his
head in his hands. On the way up we'd had to stop
twice at gas stations when he thought he might have
to use a rest room.

"You all right?" I called.

"It's okay, it's okay," he said, but when I tried
afterward to get him to take a little stroll around the
grounds with me, he said he was afraid to walk outside in case he needed to go to the toilet. He still
hadn't moved his bowels, and he asked me to drive
over to buy some prune juice at the general store to
see if that would help. He was dreadfully down, mentally and physically depleted, though once, when I
happened to be in the hall outside the living room,
where he sat, shrunken-looking, in the easy chair in
front of the fireplace, I heard him muttering some-

thing that turned out not to be about his own misery at all. "That poor Chinaman," he was saying.

The next morning he was stronger at breakfast and was even able to drink some tepid tea and to tolerate in his mouth about half of the.bowl of oatmeal that Claire had prepared for him and cooled with some milk. I went up to his bedroom while they were talking at the table—patiently Claire listened as he told her, and not for the first time either, what a saint his mother had been, cooking for eight, nine, and ten people, taking in immigrant relatives who arrived penniless at their door, scrubbing the outside wooden staircase on her knees . . . I intended to air his room, make the bed for him, and collect the soiled things from his hospital suitcase and take them over to the laundry that afternoon with our week's wash. But when I pulled back the top sheet of his bed, I saw that the bottom sheet was stained with his blood and so was the seat of his fresh pajamas. I threw his pajamas into the laundry hamper, got him a clean pair of my own, and then stripped the bed and made it up fresh. Where his midsection would lie, I stretched a double thickness of heavy bath towels across the width of the bed to prevent him from staining the bottom sheet again. I was alarmed by the evidence of so much rectal bleeding and didn't know how to account for it. I wondered if he did.

I had no chance to find out, because immediately after he had finished talking to Claire—while cleaning up the breakfast dishes, she'd heard the details of the bankruptcy of the little shoe store he'd opened up with my mother after their marriage—he took the newspaper from the day before and went up again to the bathroom. He'd had a glass of prune juice before retiring and another at breakfast, but when I called in to him some twenty minutes later to ask if he was all right, he replied glumly, like somebody at the Off-Track Betting parlor instead of on the toilet, "No luck."

"It'll happen," I called back.

"Four days," he said, mournfully.

"The biopsy, the anesthetic, lying in the bed—everything's thrown your system off. Another day or two of regular meals, a little exercise, and you'll be fine. How about coming outside? Seth and Ruth will be here any minute. Walk over with me to my studio and you can sit on the porch while I answer my mail."

"In a little while."

He didn't emerge for another half hour, and then looking so thoroughly defeated that it wasn't necessary to ask anything. Downstairs he said no to a walk and sank down in the living room easy chair again. I sat on the sofa with the *Times* and offered to read to him about Dukakis and Bush. "Bush," he said disgustedly, "and his boss, Mr. Ray-gun. You know what he learned to do in eight years, Mr. Ray-gun? Sleep and salute. The greatest saluter in the country. I never saw a better saluter." I began to read to him

from the front page of the *Times*, but he interrupted
to tell me that he had left his teeth upstairs and that
he didn't want "the children" to see him without
them. So I set down the paper and went upstairs to
get them from the shelf beside the toilet, where he'd
put them while he was trying in vain to move his
bowels. Under the tap, I rinsed the teeth of the remains of his breakfast and then carried them downstairs, thinking, "His teeth, his eyes, his face, his
bowels, his rectum, his brain . . ." and there was
plenty more left. It could be worse and it would be
worse, much worse, but this was still a pretty healthy
lot of misery for the beginning of an end. It probably
wouldn't even have been inappropriate for that poor
Chinaman lying in his bed and choking on his tube
to think, in passing, about my father, "That poor
Jew."

We had lunch in the summer room, just off the
kitchen, a rustic, big, barnlike room with a stone
floor that originally had been the woodshed of the old
farmhouse. One side of the room was now all sliding
glass doors and looked off to the lawn, the stone
walls, and the meadows and fields that opened out in
front of the house. In the past I used to set him up
there in a wicker chair facing the view, and in warm
weather he could sit all morning contentedly reading
the daily *Times*, the news about Israel first and then
the articles about the Reagan administration that en-

abled him to stoke up his hatred of the president for
the rest of the day.

Now, with Seth and Ruth visiting for lunch, and
all of us making light conversation, and the luminous
day as seductive as a summer's day gets, he was
utterly isolated within a body that had become a ter-
rifying escape-proof enclosure, the holding pen in a
slaughterhouse.

Near the end of lunch he pushed back his chair
and started toward the steps to the kitchen. It was
the third time during the meal that he had got up to
leave the table, and I got up with him to help him
upstairs. He wouldn't let me help, however, and
since I figured he was setting off to try yet again to
move his bowels, I didn't want to embarrass him by
insisting.

We were drinking our coffee when it occurred
to me that he was still gone. I quietly left the table
and, while the others were talking, slipped into the
house, certain that he was dead.

He wasn't, though he might well have been
wishing that he were.

I smelled the shit halfway up the stairs to the
second floor. When I got to his bathroom, the door
was ajar, and on the floor of the corridor outside the
bathroom were his dungarees and his undershorts.
Standing inside the bathroom door was my father,
completely naked, just out of the shower and drip-
ping wet. The smell was overwhelming.

At the sight of me he came close to bursting into

tears. In a voice as forlorn as any I had ever heard, from him or anyone, he told me what it hadn't been difficult to surmise. "I beshat myself," he said.

The shit was everywhere, smeared underfoot on the bathmat, running over the toilet bowl edge and, at the foot of the bowl, in a pile on the floor. It was splattered across the glass of the shower stall from which he'd just emerged, and the clothes discarded in the hallway were clotted with it. It was on the corner of the towel he had started to dry himself with. In this smallish bathroom, which was ordinarily mine, he had done his best to extricate himself from his mess alone, but as he was nearly blind and just up out of a hospital bed, in undressing himself and getting into the shower he had managed to spread the shit over everything. I saw that it was even on the tips of the bristles of my toothbrush hanging in the holder over the sink.

"It's okay," I said, "it's okay, everything is going to be okay."

I reached into the shower stall and turned the water back on and fiddled with the taps until it was the right temperature. Taking the towel out of his hand, I helped him back under the shower.

"Take the soap and start from scratch," I said, and while he obediently began again to soap his body all over, I gathered his clothes and the towels and the bathmat together in a heap and went down the hall to the linen closet and got a pillowcase to dump them in. I also found a fresh bath towel for him. Then

I got him out of the shower and took him straight into the hallway where the floor was still clean, and wrapped him up in the towel and began to dry him. "You made a valiant effort," I said, "but I'm afraid it was a no-win situation."

"I beshat myself," he said, and this time he dissolved in tears.

I got him into his bedroom, where he sat on the edge of the bed and continued to towel himself while I went off and got a terry-cloth robe of mine. When he was dry I helped him into the robe and then pulled back the top sheet of the bed and told him to get in and take a nap.

"Don't tell the children," he said, looking up at me from the bed with his one sighted eye.

"I won't tell anyone," I said. "I'll say you're taking a rest."

"Don't tell Claire."

"Nobody," I said. "Don't worry about it. It could have happened to anyone. Just forget about it and get a good rest."

I lowered the shades to darken the room and closed the door behind me.

The bathroom looked as though some spiteful thug had left his calling card after having robbed the house. As my father was tended to and he was what counted, I would just as soon have nailed the door shut and forgotten that bathroom forever. "It's like writing a book," I thought—"I have no idea where to begin." But I stepped gingerly across the floor and

reached out and threw open the window, which was
a start. Then I went down the back stairway to the
kitchen, and keeping out of sight of Seth and Ruth
and Claire, who were still in the summer room talking, I got a bucket, a brush, and a box of Spic and
Span from the cabinet under the sink and two rolls
of paper towels and came back upstairs to the bathroom.

Where his shit lay in front of the toilet bowl in
what was more or less a contiguous mass, it was
easiest to get rid of. Just scoop it up and flush it
away. And the shower door and the windowsill and
the sink and the soap dish and the light fixtures and
the towel bars were no problem. Lots of paper towels
and lots of soap. But where it had lodged in the narrow, uneven crevices of the floor, between the wide
old chestnut planks, I had my work cut out for me.
The scrub brush seemed only to make things worse,
and eventually I took down my toothbrush and, dip-
ping it in and out of the bucket of hot sudsy water,
proceeded inch by inch, from wall to wall, one crev-
ice at a time, until the floor was as clean as I could
get it. After some fifteen minutes on my knees, I
decided that flecks and particles down so deep that I
still couldn't reach them we would simply all live
with. I removed the curtain from the window, even
though it looked to be clean, and shoved it in the
pillowcase with all the other soiled things, and then
I went into Claire's bathroom and got some eau de
cologne, which I sprinkled freely over the swabbed

and scoured room, flicking it off my fingertips like
holy water. I set up a small summer fan in one corner
and got it going, and I went back to Claire's bathroom and washed my arms and my hands and my
face. There was a little shit in my hair, so I washed
that out, too.

I tiptoed back into the bedroom where he was
asleep, still breathing, still living, still with me—yet
another setback outlasted by this man whom I had
known unendingly as my father. I felt awful about
his heroic, hapless struggle to cleanse himself before
I had got up to the bathroom and about the shame of
it, the disgrace he felt himself to be, and yet now that
it was over and he was so deep in sleep, I thought I
couldn't have asked anything more for myself before
he died—this, too, was right and as it should be. You
clean up your father's shit because it has to be
cleaned up, but in the aftermath of cleaning it up,
everything that's there to feel is felt as it never was
before. It wasn't the first time that I'd understood
this either: once you sidestep disgust and ignore nau-
sea and plunge past those phobias that are fortified
like taboos, there's an awful lot of life to cherish.

Though maybe once is enough, I added, ad-
dressing myself mentally to the sleeping brain
squeezed in by the cartilaginous tumor; if I have to
do this every day, I may not wind up feeling quite so
thrilled.

I carried the stinking pillowcase downstairs and
put it into a black garbage bag which I tied shut, and

I carried the bag out to the car and dumped it in the trunk to take to the laundry. And *why* this was right and as it should be couldn't have been plainer to me, now that the job was done. So *that* was the patrimony. And not because cleaning it up was symbolic of something else but because it wasn't, because it was nothing less or more than the lived reality that it was.

There was my patrimony: not the money, not the tefillin, not the shaving mug, but the shit.

I helped him bathe the next night. That morning, making up his bed, I had again found blood stains on his pajama trousers and on the layer of bath towels covering the bottom sheet, and when I'd asked if he was aware of all that blood, he told me that it was what happened when he didn't take a sitz bath before going to sleep. "But if that's all it is, you can bathe in the front bathroom," I said. "You should have told me. You don't have to take a shower."

"I need Epsom salts."

I drove to the drugstore in the next town to get a box of Epsom salts, and that evening I drew him a bath and stirred a handful into the water. I sat on the edge of the tub while the water ran, testing the temperature with my fingers—my mother, I remembered, used to test it with her elbow. He sat waiting on the lowered toilet seat in my red terry-cloth robe. When the tub was full, I put the rubberized shower mat on the tub floor to guard against his taking a fall getting in and out. Then I offered my arm, but he

wouldn't let me help him even when I insisted. Instead, he made me stand aside, and by kneeling and
swiveling about, he managed to get one leg into the
water and then the other and, once inside, to circle
around slowly on his knees until he was facing the
front.

"That's a complicated maneuver," I said.

"I do this all alone at night."

"Well, I'll just sit here. In case you need me."

"Ah, it feels good," he said, pushing water over
his chest with his two hands. Weakly at first, then
more vigorously, he began to flex his knees and I
could see the muscles working in his thin shanks. I
looked at his penis. I don't believe I'd seen it since
I was a small boy, and back then I used to think it
was quite big. It turned out that I had been right. It
was thick and substantial and the one bodily part that
didn't look at all old. It looked pretty serviceable.
Stouter around, I noticed, than my own. "Good for
him," I thought. "If it gave some pleasure to him and
my mother, all the better." I looked at it intently, as
though for the very first time, and waited on the
thoughts. But there weren't any more, except my
reminding myself to fix it in my memory for when he
was dead. It might prevent him from becoming ethe-
really attenuated as the years went by. "I must remember accurately," I told myself, "remember
everything accurately so that when he is gone I can
re-create the father who created me." *You must not
forget anything.*

He was kicking his legs forcefully up and down

now, rather like a baby playing in the water, but
there was nothing of a baby's delight in his grimly
set half-face. He seemed in deadly earnest about
this bath, as though, like nearly everything of late,
it, too, must be undertaken with the utmost deter-
mination.

I washed his back for him, and while I was no-
ticing how pale his body had become, he said, "That
happened to me one other time in my life."

I understood what he was alluding to and just
kept soaping away with the cloth, as though scrubbing at him like this might renew some of the vigor.

"It was after I was transferred to South Jersey,"
he told me. "I just took over the Maple Shade district. I had forty men down there. Big office. Twelve
secretaries. I got a phone call in the middle of the
night that there was somebody in the office—somebody, they said, broke into the office. I got out of
bed, and before I could make it to the toilet, the same
thing happened. Must have been the fear."

"Here," I said, and gave him the soap and the
washcloth and sat back on the lowered toilet seat
while he gently washed his backside. Then with a
hand on each side of his buttocks he held his cheeks
apart. "The doctor told me to do this," he said.

"Fine," I said. "It's a good idea. Take your
time."

In 1956, at exactly my age, my father had been
entrusted by Metropolitan Life with an office of forty
agents, assistant managers, and ordinary represen-

tatives and a secretarial staff of twelve. He was a
manager who drove his employees as unsparingly as
he drove himself, and the transfer to the Maple
Shade district had been his third promotion since
1948, when he'd been elevated from an assistant
manager in Newark. What these promotions meant
was that he was given responsibility for a larger office
with a greater potential for increasing his income but
in even worse shape and doing less business than the
previous office, which he had rescued from its difficulties and whipped into one of the most productive
in the territory. For him advancement was generally
a kind of demotion as well, and the struggle was
perpetually uphill.

As I sat watching him let the warm water soothe
the rectal fissures that he had told me caused his
bleeding, I was thinking that the Metropolitan Life
Insurance Company could never sufficiently have
recognized what it was they had in Herman Roth.
They had rewarded him with a decent enough pension on his retirement twenty-three years before, and
during his working life he had received numerous
plaques and scrolls and lapel buttons attesting to his
achievement. Scores of managers must, of course,
have worked as hard and with no less success, but of
the thousand Metropolitan district managers scat-
tered around the country there simply could not have
been another who, on being notified in the middle of
the night that his office had been broken into, had—
to use his word—"beshat" himself out of fear. For

that kind of fealty, the company should have beati-
fied Herman Roth, as the Church beatifies martyrs
who suffer for its cause.

And had I, as his son, received devotion any less
primitive and slavish? Not always the most en-
lightened devotion—indeed, devotion from which I
already wanted to be disentangled by the time I was
sixteen and feeling myself beginning to be disfigured
by it, but devotion that I now found gratifying to be
able to requite somewhat by sitting on the lid of the
toilet overseeing him as he kicked his legs up and
down like a baby in a bassinet.

You can say that it doesn't mean much for a son
to be tenderly protective of a father once the father
is powerless and nearly destroyed. I can only reply
that I felt as protective of his vulnerability (as an
emotional family man vulnerable to family friction,
as a breadwinner vulnerable to financial uncertainty,
as a rough-hewn son of Jewish immigrants vulnerable
to social prejudice) when I was still at home and he
was powerfully healthy and driving me crazy with
advice that was useless and strictures that were
pointless and reasoning that caused me, all alone in
my room, to smack my forehead and howl in despair.
This was exactly the discrepancy that had made re-
pudiating his authority such an oppressive conflict,
as laden with grief as it was with scorn. He wasn't
just any father, he was *the* father, with everything
there is to hate in a father and everything there is to
love.

The next day, when Lil phoned from Elizabeth to ask how he was doing, I overheard him saying to her, "Philip is like a mother to me."

I was surprised. I would have thought he'd say "like a father to me," but his description was, in fact, more discriminating than my commonplace expectations while at the same time much more flagrant, unblinking, and enviably, unself-consciously blunt. Yes, he was always teaching me something, not the conventional American dad stuff, not the school stuff or the sports stuff or the Prince Charming stuff, but something coarser than could be accommodated by my predictably vainglorious boyhood yearnings for a judicious, dignified father to replace the undereducated father who I found myself half-ashamed of at the very same time that his assailability, particularly as a target of anti-Semitic discrimination, quickened my solidarity with him and hardened my hatred of his belittlers: he taught me the vernacular. He *was* the vernacular, unpoetic and expressive and point-blank, with all the vernacular's glaring limitations and all its durable force.

Anti-Semitism had, in fact, been the subject of a brief exchange, only the previous fall, between John Creedon, the president and C.E.O. of Metropolitan Life, and me as a result of an autobiographical piece that I'd published in the *New York Times Book Review* in October. The piece, which, as "Safe at

Home," became the opening chapter of *The Facts*, described my Newark neighborhood as a protective sanctuary for the Jewish children who grew up there during the thirties and forties, when I for one had felt menaced, as an American, by the Germans and the Japanese and, though only a child, "was not unaware," as a Jew, "of the power to intimidate that emanated from the highest and lowest reaches of gentile America."

It was an allusion that I'd made there to the corporate discrimination practiced by Metropolitan Life in those years that was singled out by John Creedon in his letter. After reminding me that he had met my father several years earlier, Creedon went on to tell me that my father had said nothing to him on that occasion about any such discrimination; and he was certainly confident, Creedon continued, that no discrimination of any sort existed at the Metropolitan today. What had actually prompted him to write, he said, was a letter, taking exception to my *Times* piece, from an old associate of his, a retired M.D. who had been an officer of the company in the 1940s. Along with his own letter, Creedon enclosed the correspondence I had unwittingly instigated between the two of them.

The doctor's letter to Creedon devoted three paragraphs to refuting my characterization of the Metropolitan as discriminatory during the thirties and forties. He told Creedon that he was "shocked" that Philip Roth should believe this and, as evidence to the contrary, noted that "one of the best known senior officers of the Metropolitan was a Jew, Louis I. Dublin, world-famous for his public health and statistical pronouncements in the name of Metropolitan," and that another Jew, Lee Frankel, was "a senior officer and virtually the right-hand man of Haley Fisk," the company president. "I suppose," he went on, "Mr. Roth will say in his defense that these are his childhood impressions and perhaps he is just reflecting comments and attitudes expressed at home about the Company. I wish there were some way to try to correct these impressions."

In Creedon's reply to the doctor he mentioned having invited my father to come to the home office to have lunch with him some years back, after having run into my brother at a Chicago dinner party and been told about our father's career at the Metropolitan, his starting out as a lowly agent for them and ending up the district manager of a sizable office. Creedon described my father as an interesting person and added that if the views he'd once held about the Metropolitan's religious bias were accurately reported in his son's autobiography, they had clearly changed since.

If the doctor was shocked that I should think that a great American insurance company had ever discriminated against Jews, I was myself not a little surprised that two of that company's eminent executives, whose letters were otherwise wholly well-meaning, should find this simple historical fact had

still to be denied in the late 1980s, even to themselves. However, had there been nothing more an-
noying in these letters than this unlikely innocence,
I probably would have responded with a cordial note
saying that I had reason to hold a different opinion,
and ended it there. What rankled me and goaded me
on was that they were both determined to blame an
unflattering perception of their company on my father, on unsubstantiated "attitudes" and "views" of
his rather than on the company's prior practices.

I phoned my father after getting these letters
and said to him, "Hey, you were wrong all those
years about the Metropolitan. They loved Jews.
Couldn't promote them fast enough. All that other
stuff was just Jew paranoia."

I read him the letter that the doctor had written
to John Creedon in response to my piece.

When I was finished, he began to laugh a little
sardonically.

"Well, what do you think?" I said.

"The guy's wet behind the ears. What's his
name again?"

I told him.

"Sure Dublin was a Jew," he said. "So was my
boss, Peterfreund. But for a Jew to advance in that
company like a Christian? In those days? Come on.
You could count the Jews in the home office and you
wouldn't need your whole hand."

I spent the next few afternoons in the archives
of the American Jewish Committee on East Fifty-

sixth Street. I'd been directed there by one of the
officers of the B'nai Brith Anti-Defamation League,
when I'd phoned the A.D.L. to ask where I might do
research on discrimination in the insurance industry.
After I'd compiled pages of notes drawn from articles
published over the years in the *New York Times*, from
memos of the Civil Rights Section of the A.J.C., and
from various books and periodicals, I composed a
two-and-a-half-page letter to John Creedon, provid-
ing documentation for those "attitudes" of my father's which he and the doctor had been so quick to
discredit.

December 10, 1987

Dear Mr. Creedon:

. . . I'm sure, as you suggest in your letter, that the avail-
ability of executive opportunities to minority groups has
vastly expanded at the Metropolitan since the 1930s and
1940s, the period I was writing about in my autobiographical essay. Since the passage of the Fair Employment
Practice Act in 1951, there has, of course, been steady
and successful pressure on business and industries previously discriminatory, to recruit, hire, and promote to
managerial and executive positions members of minority
groups. Nonetheless, as late as the 1960s, the federal
government—according to a *New York Times* article of
March 20, 1966—had to start "a quiet but seemingly firm
campaign against alleged religious discrimination in insurance companies." "The aim," the story said, "is to
open executive positions to Jews and Roman Catholics,
as well as to Negroes and other racial minorities, in com-

panies where the top jobs may be reserved for Anglo-
Saxon Protestants."

I went on to quote from an investigation into the
insurance industry published in 1966 by New York
State Attorney General Louis Lefkowitz and from a
study made in 1960, while my father happened still
to be working for the Metropolitan, which indicated
that in the home offices of the seven major life insurance companies the proportion of Jewish executives
was about three and a half percent of the combined
seven companies and that two thirds of those were
confined, like Louis I. Dublin, largely to statistical
work or employed as actuaries, physicians, attor-
neys, or accountants. I ended by saying, "In the light
of what all these findings reveal about discriminatory
practices in the history of the major American insurance companies . . . I wonder why it should be my
father's 'views' that you hope have changed: the historical facts do not allow for a revision of his views.
What's been called for has been a revision of insurance company policy as regards minority groups, and
this, in fact, has occurred in response to federal law
and government inquiries."

I sent a copy to Creedon and, when I saw him
next, gave a copy to my father.

After he read it, he didn't seem to know what to
make of what I had done.

"How do you find all this stuff?" he asked me.

"The archives at the American Jewish Committee. I spent a couple of afternoons there."

"He's an awfully nice fellow, Mr. Creedon. He had me to the home office for lunch, you know."

"I know."

"He sent a limousine over here to take me to the home office that day."

"Look, I'm sure he's a nice fellow. There are just a couple of little holes in his sense of history."

"Well, you laid it out for him, all right."

"Well, I didn't like what he wrote about you— that he hoped *you'd* changed *your* mind. Screw that."

"They've been awfully good to me, the Metropolitan. You know how much pension I've received since I retired? I figured it out here just last week. Well over a quarter of a million dollars."

"That's peanuts. You're worth twice that."

"With an eighth-grade education? Am I?" He laughed. "I had nothing, absolutely nothing. Mother and I were flat broke and they hired me. It's a wonder what happened to a man like me."

"The hell it is. You worked. You sweated blood for them. You have a history and so do they. The difference is that you own up to yours, you say you were 'nothing,' but they don't like to admit to theirs, if those letters are any indication."

"They don't like the truth. What's so unusual about that? Do me a favor, will you? After this," he said, holding up my letter, "that's enough."

Well, *this* was new—my father expressing cha-
grin over something I had written. In my Zuckerman
novels, I had given Nathan Zuckerman a father who
could not stand his writer son's depiction of Jewish
characters, whereas fate had given me a fiercely
loyal and devoted father who had never found a thing
in my books to criticize—what enraged *him* were the
Jews who attacked my books as anti-Semitic and
self-hating. No, what made my father nervous wasn't
what I wrote about Jews but, as it turned out, what I
had now written about Gentiles—about Gentiles to
Gentiles, and to Gentiles who had been his bosses.

"I don't think they're going to tamper with your
pension because of my letter—if that's what's worrying you."

"Nothing's worrying me," he said.

"I certainly didn't mean to upset you. Quite the
contrary."

"I'm not upset. But just don't send 'em another
one."

And yet, at my father's funeral, my cousin Ann
told me that when she and her husband, Peter, had
been visiting him one evening, he had gone to his
files and taken out the letter to show it proudly to
Peter, who was his lawyer. To me he never mentioned it again, nor did I receive a reply from anyone
at the Metropolitan.

He was with us in Connecticut for a week after the
biopsy, and by the time he was ready to return to

Elizabeth there was very little pain in his mouth and
he was able to eat again with appetite; he had gained
back the few pounds that he'd lost in the hospital and
even recovered enough strength to take a short walk
with me after breakfast and again in the afternoon.
Every morning he came into the kitchen saying,
"Slept like a top," and in the evening, after dinner,
he sat across from Claire with his coffee, and long
after I had slipped away to read or to watch the ball
game, he was still in the kitchen narrating his stories
to her about the family and their fortunes in America.
They were tedious stories, to anyone who had grown
up outside the family largely pointless stories, and,
one would have assumed, by now tremendously rep-
etitious even to him (this one died, this one married,
this one lost his money, this one lost his wife, this
one, thank God, finally did okay). Yet he recited
them night after night, with no less freshness than
Yul Brynner singing " 'Tis a Puzzlement" in *The King
and I* for the four thousandth time. Every night at
the kitchen table Claire sat and listened, drooping
with boredom but by no means unimpressed by the
urgency with which this meandering saga unfolded
or by the hypnotic hold that the mundane destiny of
an ordinary immigrant family seemed still to have on
him in his eighty-seventh year. How his late brother
Charlie, who'd died in 1936, married Fanny Spitzer
in 1912; how, after Fanny died fourteen years later,
Charlie married Sophie Lasker; how Sophie was a
mother to Milton, Rhoda, Kenny, and Jeanette; how,
in 1942, only twenty-eight years old, Jeanette died;

how his brother Morris, the go-getting, prosperous
brother who died at twenty-nine, had a shoelace factory down on Pacific Street, where my grandfather
used to put tips on the shoelaces; how Morris had
two houses and four garages; how when he died he
left his fortune behind to a spendthrift wife, who
after Morris's death bought a Velie. "You ever hear
of the Velie automobile? Look it up. V-e-l-i-e. It was
a big roadster. Everything went, Ella sold everything.
Then she got married again. She married a guy and
he impregnated her and she thought she had a lump
in her stomach. And this guy was an Army captain,
and he took all her money, Morris's fortune, and he
went to Germany, he made her buy leather—but her
father, Uncle Klein, said they had to pay the money
to an American bank and he wouldn't give up the bill
of lading. Uncle Klein used to have a five-and-ten-
cent store on the corner of Avon Avenue—no, Clinton Avenue, Clinton and Hunterdon Street—" It was
his Deuteronomy, the history of his Israel, and ever
since his retirement, whether he was on a Caribbean
cruise or in a Florida hotel lobby or in a doctor's
waiting room, very few who wound up sitting across
from him for any length of time didn't get at least the
abridged version of his sacred text. Gentiles whom
he had sometimes run into in his travels with my
mother had been known to pick themselves up and
move off in mid-sentence, and even on those occasions when my mother dared to explain to him why a
perfect stranger might not be interested in Charlie's

Belmont Avenue shoe store or Morris's motion picture theater next door to the shoelace factory on Pacific Street, he never seemed to get the idea, or to
want to. All the privation and rebuilding and regen-
eration, all those *people*, all that *dying*, all their *work*
—how could anyone fail to be moved and even, ultimately, to be as awestruck as he was by how, in
America, our Roths had persevered and endured?

At the end of the week I drove him home to
Elizabeth, stopping first in Manhattan to take him to
the ophthalmologist. We had decided that there was
nothing to do now but forget the tumor and proceed
with the eye operation. He was to have a preoperative examination that afternoon and was scheduled
to go back into the hospital at the beginning of July,
after the holiday weekend, for the removal of the
cataract. My brother was flying in to see him through
that.

As he was ninety percent blind in the right eye,
the operation on the other eye was going to render
him virtually sightless, the doctor told us, for perhaps as long as three or four weeks. We had very
little time to find somebody to look after him during
his convalescence, but fortunately, after only a day
or two of phoning around, I discovered that my
brother's former housekeeper, Ingrid Burlin, who for
five years had helped Sandy raise his two boys after
his first wife died of cancer in 1971, was just com-
pleting a job with a Manhattan family. Ingrid was
willing to begin working for us the day he got home

from the cataract operation and to continue on until he left with Lil in December for their four months in West Palm Beach (if the tumor spared him for West Palm Beach). Ingrid was now in her forties, an exceedingly good-natured, intelligent, and reliable woman to whom both my mother and my father had grown very close during the years she'd been with my brother, and it seemed a piece of astonishing good luck that she should be available to look after him at just this moment. Ingrid was to come in on the bus from Manhattan for eight hours a day, five or six days a week, to cook for him, shop for him, keep the apartment clean for him, and, what afforded us the most relief, keep him company all day while he was housebound. Since Sandy and I knew that our father wasn't about to dip into his CDs or his savings accounts in order to pay Ingrid's salary, we agreed to divide the cost between us and to reimburse ourselves from the bequest after his death. There was enough money there to pay Ingrid for three years, if, as was unlikely, he remained alive that long.

On the drive down, when I saw that his spirits had begun to plummet now that the week with us was over and everything loomed up just as overwhelmingly as it had before, I reminded him that Ingrid's presence was going to make a big difference —as was the cataract operation. What with Ingrid around the house and his sight restored, he would be far less dependent on Lil, and perhaps the tension between them that his illness had exacerbated would become manageable again.

But saying that got him going in a way I hadn't foreseen. "Suddenly she's a Jew," he said to me. "I had to drag her to services. Till she knew me she never went at all. Lil didn't even know where the synagogue *was*. But the Friday before my operation she left me to go to services. I told her, 'Even a dog stands by his master. People buy a dog for companionship, and you run away from me!' "

"Well," I said, "a dog might not have been the best example. I can see where she might not feel flattered by the comparison."

But he was in no mood to be either amused or mollified. He was, rather, in the mood to hate, now that he was headed home. I wondered if some of what he expressed might not be veiled hatred of me for taking him home. Or maybe he was furious over that question he had not bothered to ask Dr. Benjamin or Dr. Meyerson or me, the writer son, because he knew that none of us, even with all our schooling, our degrees, our smooth sentences and clever words, could make any more sense of it than he did. Why should a man die? It was enough to put anybody in a rage, that question. He was indispensable, goddamnit, if no longer to others then to himself. So why should he die? Someone with brains answer that!

"She doesn't do anything right," he told me.

"Who does?"

"Mother did. Mother did everything right."

"Well, that made her pretty much the only one in the world then. Maybe you better get off Lil's back."

"Look, there are plenty of women down in Florida who I could move in with. They're crazy about my company."

I couldn't be cruel enough, a moment earlier, to remind him that my mother, who may have looked to be doing everything right when he was away at the office ten and twelve hours a day, hadn't seemed so perfect to him during the last years of her life. Nor could I remind him now that the Bal Harbour women whom he'd wowed in 1981—back when he'd appeared in the condominium pool, freshly widowered, doing fifteen minutes of his methodical, slow breaststroke every noon and then, in his trunks and his robe, sitting in the sun telling "the girls" the jokes from the Elizabeth Y—might not be so crazy for the company of the man he was in 1988.

He didn't need me to remind him, anyway; it occurred to him spontaneously a second or two later and made him even angrier than before, this time ostensibly at Lil's sister, not a great favorite of his (nor he of hers, from what I surmised).

"Why doesn't she marry *her*?" he demanded. "They're on the phone sixteen hours a day—why doesn't she marry her sister and get it over with!"

But the one Lil had once wanted to marry was my father. Only he was married, if not to my mother any longer, to their marriage. Some time ago, in a mellower mood, he'd said to me, "I sometimes think that Mother sent Lil to me." I was surprised by this dreaminess, which was so very uncharacteristic, but

as I didn't see where it did any harm—I wondered,
even, if it might not be just the lullaby to soothe his
conscience and diminish a little the shame and guilt
perpetuating his fidelity to a corpse—I said, "Who
knows? Maybe she did." He'd seemed to be trying to
find a way not so much to loving Lil wholeheartedly
(even he was too experienced to expect that) as to
granting her a position of equality in his distinctive
clan, with what was to him its unparalleled history.
He had always been wonderfully attentive and devoted to any friend who was ill, and probably never
came closer to being a loving husband than when he
supported Lil, over the period of a year, through two
mastectomies and afterward helped nurse her back
to health. But only as his patient did she get anywhere near being a darling wife; and once *he* began
to falter, once he became increasingly needy himself,
she was doomed by being imperfect never to achieve
the status of Bess Roth, whom he now exalted, along
with his mother, as a paragon of womanhood. With
Lil, once the romantic infatuation had waned, he
lived out the less censored version of what he had
done with my mother, particularly toward the end.

Temporarily worn down by the rush of rage, he
soon let his head slump forward and fell asleep.
When he awoke, on Route 684, the object of his fury
was drivers and driving. Somebody changed lanes in
front of me, he said disgustedly, "What the hell is
that guy doing?" Somebody whizzed past me on my
left, he cried, "Doesn't anybody observe the fifty-

five-mile limit anymore?" Then: "These goddamn trucks!" Then: "Smoking! She's got a baby in the car and she's smoking!"

"Take it easy," I said.

"Now they've got the telephones. There's a brilliant invention. They drive and they talk on the telephone! Maybe Ingrid can help out Abe," he suddenly said to me.

"What? What are you talking about?"

"Maybe Ingrid can help out Abe," he repeated. "Abe lives with a terrible bitch."

Abe was a ninety-three-year-old neighbor with whom my father tried to take a daily constitutional when the weather was good. Abe appeared to be quite alert and moved with an amazingly upright, confident gait for a man that old, though when he and my father went off in the afternoon to take their turn around the block, they linked arms to be sure that neither of them tripped on the cracked cement of the local sidewalks. "The halt and the blind" my father called the pair of them, wryly. Sometimes they went down North Broad Street as far as the drugstore, sometimes they accompanied each other to the barbershop, and one day when I drove over, they'd just come back from going to vote together in the mayoral primary. The results of the primary were a foregone conclusion, my father told me, but voting had given him and Abe something to do. And whenever they returned from wherever they had been and Abe went on to his own apartment, my father invariably said, "Five minutes from now he'll forget he saw me."

The day I'd gone over to tell him about the tumor, Abe had called just after I'd broken the bad news, while my father was compressed down in a corner of the sofa contemplating what he was in for. I got up and answered the phone and there was Abe on the other end, a real zing in his sprightly voice. "Hello, Herman?" "No, Philip," I said. "Your father want to take a walk?" "He wants to sit and talk now, Abe. Maybe he'll go out later." Barely ten minutes had passed when the phone rang again. "Your father want to take a walk?" "No, Abe, not right now, I'm afraid." And after I'd hung up for the second time, I left the receiver off the hook just as I had the night before my mother's funeral, when Wilkins, another neighbor, was trying to spook my father with his crazy laugh.

"What's Ingrid's number in New York? I'm going to talk to her about Abe."

"Dad, leave Abe as he is, okay? For the time being let's have Ingrid help just you."

"Once I get this damn eye fixed—! If I could see, I could go to the bank, I could go to the dentist, I wouldn't need anybody."

"Well, you're going to have it fixed in a couple of weeks. David Krohn moved heaven and earth to get you scheduled as soon as possible. It's why we're going to see him today."

"When Aunt Millie died, Ann called me and I

just broke down and wept on the phone with her for
half an hour. Did I tell you that?"

Ann, you remember, was the daughter of my
mother's younger sister Millie.

"I wept for half an hour," he said. "And you
know who I realize I was weeping for? Mother. When
she died, I ran around the hospital shouting,
'Where's my wife? What are you doing for my wife?'
I didn't have time to cry, I was so angry. But when I
heard Millie died, that was the last part of Mother,
and I cried like a baby."

We were entering Manhattan from the West
Side Highway when he awakened from sleeping for
the third time and, resigned and sounding rather
sheepish, said, "Maybe Ingrid can look after me for
good."

"That's possible, too," I said.

6

***They Fought
Because They Were Fighters,
and They Fought Because
They Were Jews***

Just about a year passed before he began, all at
once, to lose his equilibrium. In the meantime, he'd
had the cataract removed—restoring to his left eye
practically 20/20 vision—and he and Lil had gone to
Florida for their usual stay of four months. In December, in Palm Beach, they even attended the wedding that Sandy Kuvin had invited him to the

previous spring, back when the brain surgeon had
told me that unless we okayed the operation, in a
relatively short time he'd be much worse off—back
when I thought that he'd never see Florida again.

When he returned to Elizabeth at the end of
March and I went over to welcome him home, I saw
that his condition had already worsened since I'd
visited him in Florida the month before. His head
was beginning to hurt him practically every day, the
facial paralysis seemed to have got worse, causing
his speech to thicken now nearly to the point of un-
intelligibility, and he had become alarmingly un-
steady on his feet. Late one night, a few weeks after
coming home, when he got out of bed to go to the
bathroom, he lost his balance (or momentarily
blacked out) and fell. He was on the bathroom floor
some ten minutes before Lil woke up and heard him
calling. He came away with nothing worse than some
badly bruised ribs, but the damage to his morale was
enormous.

At about this time, a friend told me about a living will, a legal document that—in its own phraseol-
ogy—enables you to declare in advance that in the
event of extreme physical or mental disability from
which there's no reasonable expectation of recovery,
you refuse any sort of life-support system. The signer
designates who will make the necessary medical
treatment decisions if he or she is incapable of doing
so. I called my lawyer to ask if living wills were valid
in New Jersey, and when she said yes, I instructed

her to draw up two living wills, one for my father and another for me.

The next week I drove over to New Jersey to have dinner with my father, Lil, and Ingrid, who was working as his housekeeper again now that he was home—she'd begun the previous July, just after he'd had the cataract removed. I brought with me my own living will, signed and notarized at a local luncheonette that afternoon, and the living will that had been prepared by my lawyer for him, which assigned the power to make medical decisions—if he was not able —to my brother and me. I was hoping that if I showed him that I'd had a living will drawn up for myself, signing his might seem to him not so much portentous as commonsensical, something any adult ought to do regardless of age or physical condition.

But when I got there and discovered how depressed he still was as a result of the bathroom fall, I found it was even harder for me to talk about the living will than it had been to tell him about the brain tumor the year before. In fact, I couldn't do it. Ingrid had prepared a big turkey dinner and I had brought some wine and we sat a long time at the dining table, where, instead of explaining what a living will was and why I wanted him to have one, I tried to get his mind as far from death as I could by telling him about a book that I'd just finished reading. I'd picked it up while browsing in a Judaica store on upper Broadway when I'd been out taking a walk a few days before. It was called *The Jewish Boxers' Hall of Fame*—old

archive photographs and chapter-long biographies of
thirty-nine boxers, a number of them world champions or "title claimants" who had been active in the
ring when my father was young. As a boy, along with
my brother, I had been taken by him to the Thursday
night fights at Newark's Laurel Garden, and though
I for one no longer had an interest in the sport, he
still enjoyed enormously watching boxing on television. I asked him how many of the old-time Jewish
fighters he thought he could name.

"Well," he said, "there was Abe Attell."

"That's right," I said. "You were just a little kid
when Attell was featherweight champ."

"Was I? I thought I saw him fight. There was
what's-his-name, the big lug . . . Levinsky—Bat-
tling Levinsky. He was champ—right?"

"Light heavyweight champ."

"Benny Leonard, of course. Ruby Goldstein. He
became a referee."

"So did Leonard. He dropped dead refereeing a
fight at the old St. Nick's Arena. Remember that?"

"No, I don't. But there was Lew Tendler. He
finally opened a restaurant. I used to go to it, in
Philadelphia. A steak house. They were terrific characters. They were poor boys, just like the colored,
that made the grade in boxing. Most of them wasted
their money, they died poor men. The only one who
I think made money was Tendler. I remember the
era very vividly of Tendler, Attell, and Leonard. Bar-
ney Ross. He was a helluva fighter. I saw him fight
in Newark. There was Bummy Davis—he was a Jew.

There was Slapsie Maxie Rosenbloom. Sure, I remember them."

"Did you know," I said, "that Slapsie Maxie
fought another Jew for the light heavyweight title?"
I'd learned this myself only the night before, skim-
ming through an appendix to the *Hall of Fame* book
titled "Jews Who Fought Other Jews for the World
Title." The list, a longer one than I would have expected, came just before the appendix listing "Lester
Bromberg's 10 Great Jewish American Boxers of All
Time." "He fought a guy named Abie Bain," I said.

"Sure. Abie Bain," my father said, "he was a
nut from Jersey here—Newark, Hillside, around
these parts. And he was a bum. They were all bums.
You know how it was: these kids grew up, they had
a tough life, the slums, no money, and they always
had an adversary. The Christian religion was an adversary. They fought two battles. They fought because they were fighters, and they fought because
they were Jews. They'd put two guys in the ring, an
Italian and a Jew, an Irishman and a Jew, and they
fought like they meant it, they fought to hurt. There
was always a certain amount of hatred in it. Trying
to show who was superior."

This line of thinking led him to remember a
childhood friend, Charlie Raskus, who, after he left
the neighborhood, became a killer for the kingpin
Newark mobster Longie Zwillman.

"Charlie was no good even as a kid," my father
said.

"How so?" I asked.

"He tied his teacher to her desk in grade school."

"No kidding."

"Sure. They threw him out and put him in an ungraded school and he wound up killing people for Longie. They were a bad bunch, Charlie and his friends. They were all Jewish boys around the Third Ward. The Polocks used to kill the Jews who had beards, in the Third Ward I'm saying, not just in the old country, and so the Jewish boys started a gang—it had a name but it doesn't come to me right away—and they'd kill the Polocks. I mean personally kill them. They were all no good. My father used to call them 'Yiddische bums.' "

"What happened to Charlie Raskus?"

"He's dead. He died. Natural causes. He wasn't that old. Even the bastards die," my father said. "That's about the only good thing you can say for death—it gets the sons of bitches, too."

About ten-thirty, after we'd caught the Mets score on the news and he seemed, at least for the moment, to have been distracted from his gloom, I took the living wills, his and mine, which I'd carried rather officially with me in something I rarely ever use—my ancient briefcase—and drove with them back to New York, thinking maybe it was a mistake to force him to face the most bitter of all possibilities. "Enough," I thought, and went home, where, unable to sleep, I passed the night studying, in Appendix V, the won-and-lost records of some fifty Jewish world champions and contenders, including Jersey's own

Abie Bain, who'd won forty-eight—thirty-one by knockout—lost eleven, and, strangely, according to this book, had thirty-one no decisions.

Early the next morning, however, before he'd begun to have a chance to be worn down by worrying, I telephoned my father and launched into my spiel: I told him how my lawyer had suggested that I ought to have a living will, how she had explained its function to me, how I had said it sounded like a good idea and had asked her, as she was preparing one for me, to draw up one for him as well. I said, "Let me read you mine. Listen." And of course, his reaction was nothing like what I'd feared it would be.

How could I have forgotten that I was dealing with somebody who'd spent a lifetime talking to people about the thing they least wanted to think about? When I was a small boy and would go with him to his office on a Saturday morning, he used to tell me, "Life insurance is the hardest thing in the world to sell. You know why? Because the only way the customer can win is if he dies." He was an old and knowledgeable expert in these contracts dealing with death, more used to them by far than I was, and as I slowly read him each sentence over the phone, he responded as matter-of-factly as if I were reading the fine-print boilerplate prose off an insurance policy.

" 'Measures of artificial life support in the face of impending death,' " I read, " 'that I specifically refuse are: (a) Electrical or mechanical resuscitation of my heart when it has stopped beating.' "

"Uh-huh," he said.

" '(b) Nasogastric tube feeding'—that's feeding through the nose—'when I am paralyzed or unable to take nourishment by mouth.' "

"Uh-huh, yeah."

" '(c) Mechanical respiration when I am no longer able to sustain my own breathing.' "

"Uh-huh."

I continued on through to where my brother and I were named as the people who should make his medical decisions for him if he became unable to do so. Then I said, "So? How does it strike you?"

"Send it over and I'll sign."

And that was it. Instead of feeling like the insurance man's son, I felt like an insurance man myself, one who'd just sold his first policy to a customer who could win only if he died.

When Claire and I went for dinner on a May Friday a few weeks later, the focus of the evening, as far as I knew, was to be Ingrid's wonderful bouillabaisse, a dish my father liked to eat but couldn't for the life of him pronounce. For convenience's sake, he had come to call it *"ballaboosteh,"* a workable and witty enough approximation since that is the Yiddish encomium for "housewife" or "homemaker," and it seemed to encapsulate both the heartiness of the fare that Ingrid was cooking up for us and the soothing managerial role she had quickly come to play in the household.

Despite his now having to hold his arms out to balance himself against the walls of the apartment when he moved from room to room—and having to take only the tiniest steps so as to keep from falling —Ingrid's presence had enormously alleviated his sense of vulnerability and thus (contrary to my naive expectations) enabled him to *increase* his criticism of Lil. I didn't think that it was possible for him to ferret out still more things that were wrong with her, but for Lil's imperfections, even with only one good eye, his vision was microscopic.

"She can't even buy a cantaloupe," he told me in disgust on the phone one morning, and because I had by then heard just about enough on the general subject of what Lil could not do, I answered, "Look, a cantaloupe is a hard thing to buy—maybe the hardest thing there is to buy, when you stop to think about it. A cantaloupe isn't an apple, you know, where you can tell from the outside what's going on inside. I'd rather buy a car than a cantaloupe—I'd rather buy a *house* than a cantaloupe. If one time in ten I come away from the store with a decent cantaloupe, I consider myself lucky. I smell it, sniff it, press both ends with my thumb, I smell another one, press down again with my thumb—eight, nine, ten cantaloupes I can go through like this before finally I settle on one and I take it home and we cut it open for dinner and the thing is tasteless and hard as a rock. I'll tell you about making a mistake with a cantaloupe: *we all do it*. We weren't *made* to buy cantaloupe. Do me a favor, Herm, get off the woman's ass, because it isn't just Lil's weakness buying a shitty cantaloupe: *it's a human weakness.* She is being persecuted by you for something that maybe one percent of the human population is able to do right—and even with half of them it's probably guesswork."

"Well," he said uncertainly, taken aback a bit by my thoroughness, "the cantaloupe is the least of it . . ." but for the time being he had no more complaints to make to me about Lil.

On the Friday evening we joined my father, Lil, Ingrid, and Seth and Ruth for dinner in Elizabeth, our centerpiece turned out to be not the bouillabaisse but a guest whose presence I hadn't known about beforehand. A little surprisingly, when our guest sat down at the table, he told me that he had already had his dinner at home with his wife. It seemed that he had been invited, like a medieval bard or a strolling player, to tell his story to us while *we* ate our dinner —to tell it particularly to me.

He was Walter Herrmann, a survivor of two concentration camps who had come to Newark in 1947, speaking only German; fresh from Auschwitz and only twenty-two, he had somehow found a little money somewhere and, with a partner, bought a small grocery store just down Chancellor Avenue from my high school. From there he had gone on to buy the whole building, then the building next door, and so on, until eventually he sold off his extensive Newark holdings in the mid-fifties—just before the

bottom began to fall out of the property market there
—went into furs—his family's business in Germany
before the war—and became a very rich man. My
father knew him from the Elizabeth Y; they used to
play cards there when my father could still drive his
car and was going to the Y three or four times a
week. He had invited him to meet me because Walter was writing a book about his wartime experience.
This was not the first time my father had put an
aspiring author in touch with me. It did not matter to
him, either, when I told him that there was absolutely nothing I could do for somebody who was writing, say, about home mortgages or annuity funds; he
would then press me for the office telephone number
of my editor friends Aaron Asher or David Rieff and,
bypassing me, deal directly with them. Some years
back, one of the manuscripts by a friend of his that
he sent to Aaron, a book about the real-estate business, went on to be published successfully by Harper
& Row, Aaron's house at the time. My father received a finder's fee, and Aaron took the two of us
out to lunch in Manhattan. After that there was no
stopping him, if there ever had been.

While we were all having a drink in the living
room before dinner—on his arrival, Walter had pre-
sented my father with a bottle of champagne—I remembered that my father had mentioned this friend
of his to me a few weeks back when I told him on the
phone that my Hunter literature class had just been
reading a book about Auschwitz—Tadeusz Borow-

ski's *This Way for the Gas, Ladies and Gentlemen*—
and another about Treblinka—Gitta Sereny's *Into
That Darkness*. My duties, over the years, as a university professor were always a little shadowy to him,
and every once in a while he would ask me what
exactly it was I taught in my classes and I would try
to explain. After I told him about the two concentration camp books, he said, "I have a friend from the
Y who was in Auschwitz. He's writing a book himself. Wonderful man." "Is he?" "Maybe you can
help him." "I have all I can do helping myself with
my own books." "But you could give him some tips."
"Dad, I don't have any. There are no tips." "What
about Aaron Asher?" "What about him?" "Has he
moved again? Is he still at that place?" "Grove?
Yes." "Gimme his number again." "Has your friend
even finished his book?" "I told you—he's writing
it." "Why don't you wait then and call up Aaron
when the book is done."

That was the last I heard of Walter and the book
until he turned up at the bouillabaisse dinner, where
my father was instructing him, "Show him, show him
your number, Walter."

We were at the table by then, and as Ingrid was
seated between my father and Walter (who had
drawn a spare chair up directly beside me) and happened just then to be explaining to Claire and Ruth,
across the table, what went into her bouillabaisse, it
was necessary for my father to speak *over* their conversation. "Show him your number!" he called again
to his friend.

Since it was a warmish night and Walter was wearing a short-sleeved shirt—his light sports jacket he'd already removed and draped over the back of his chair—he had only to rotate his wrist a little for me to be able to read the numerals on his forearm. As he did so, he said to my father, "He's seen this before, I'm sure."

True. My sister-in-law's parents were Holocaust survivors, I knew survivors in Israel, and of course, it wasn't unusual to see camp numerals on the arms of all sorts of people one came across in New York. I had also been seated among at least a dozen survivors the year before during the weeks I had attended the trial in Jerusalem of John Demjanjuk, the Treblinka guard known as Ivan the Terrible. Probably the survivor whose number had had the greatest impact on me when I saw it was the Italian writer Primo Levi. In 1986, I had traveled to Turin to do a long interview with him for the *New York Times*, and over the course of the four days together we had become mysteriously close friends—so close that when my time came to leave, Primo said, "I don't know which of us is the younger brother and which is the older brother," and we embraced emotionally as though we might never meet again. It turned out that we never did. We had spoken at length about Auschwitz, about his twelve months there as a young man and the two grave books he'd written about the camps, and this had become the heart of the interview. It was published in the *Times*'s Sunday book section just six months before Primo Levi committed

suicide by jumping from the top of the deep stairwell
in his Turin apartment building—the same stairwell
whose five flights of steps I had mounted with such
anticipation every day I went there for our talks. I
wondered if Primo Levi and Walter Herrmann could
possibly have met at Auschwitz. They would have
been about the same age and able to understand each
other in German—thinking that it might improve his
chances of surviving, Primo had worked hard at
Auschwitz to learn the language of the Master Race.
In what way did Walter account for *his* survival?
What had *he* learned? However amateurish or simply
written the book, I expected something like that to
be its subject.

Walter held what I took to be a manuscript in a
large manila envelope on his lap. During the meal he
spoke steadily into my ear, about his bourgeois childhood in Berlin, the dancing classes, the Latin stud-
ies, about his mother, who had miraculously survived
the war, and his father, whom the Nazis had mur-
dered; he spoke about his boyhood reading—
"Heine," he said, kissing the tips of his fingers in
appreciation—and let me know how much he had
loved the works of Franz Werfel. Then he told me
how he had been able to hide for several years in
Berlin before the Nazis caught up with him and sent
him first to Belsen and then to Auschwitz only
months before the war ended.

"In Berlin?" I asked. "How could you hide in
Berlin?"

"Women. With women. I was the only man left

in Berlin. I was eighteen, nineteen. All the German men were in the Army and all the Jewish men were gone. I was hidden by women." He smiled impishly. "My book is not a book like Elie Wiesel writes or Samuel Pisar. Elie Wiesel is to me a genius. I couldn't write such a tragic book. Until the camps, I had a very happy war."

Walter opened the envelope on his lap and what he withdrew was not the manuscript of his book— not that quite yet—but first something on the order of the credentials entitling him to write his book. On the linen tablecloth, beside my bouillabaisse bowl, he placed a small, worn piece of what looked like discolored parchment. It was a much-handled, much-folded identification paper that the Germans had issued to him in the late thirties. I saw that like every other Jewish male in the Third Reich, Walter Herrmann had been given by the Aryan authorities the middle name "Israel." A photograph in one corner of the document showed a boy in his late teens, slender, full-lipped, darkish, vaguely Tartar-looking, and no Adonis. A resemblance to the man on my right was still there, even though the picture was about fifty years old. But where today, in his mid-sixties, Walter seemed no less confident than any other respectable, wealthy Jersey businessman, the boy he had been back then looked like someone who would have been far more comfortable off in a corner reading Franz Werfel than as the only male left for the women of Berlin.

The black hair that grew low on his forehead in

the photograph and was styled in what looked like a
pompadour had fallen out a week after the war; he
had lost it overnight, he said, when he came down
with typhus and nearly died following the camp's
liberation. This story, which he had told about himself barely a minute or two after having been introduced to the family in the living room, was my first
indication that Walter was not one of those survivors
who prefer to keep their memories submerged.

He had an additional certificate of validation to
produce before we got to the manuscript. This, as he
explained to me, was the outer wrapping of a pack of
cigarette papers, on the inside of which he had pen-
ciled a tiny letter from Auschwitz to his mother. She
had been in hiding somewhere in Germany, and for
such a letter to have reached her would have taken
some doing. Yet clearly she had got it, saved it, and
brought it with her to America, for here it was in
New Jersey in 1989, what could have been a son's
last words in 1944.

"Pass 'em around," my father told me, and so
Walter's Third Reich ID card and his two-inch-wide
Auschwitz letter went from me to Claire, then from
Claire to Seth and Ruth, who were born, respec-
tively, in 1957 and 1961 and who seemed as bemused
by the two documents as they were by the loquacious
stranger with the number on his arm. They passed
them on to Lil, who said of the picture, "Walter, you
look like a real *yeshiva bucher*," and she passed them
on to my father, who said, "I saw it at the Y," and

he passed them on to practical-minded Ingrid, who examined each document altogether neutrally, as though what she held in her hand had been handed over to her as identification for a check to be cashed. Finally the two documents were returned to their owner, who slipped them back in the envelope and extracted next still not the pages of manuscript but a series of recent Polaroid photographs of his grandchildren at one of their birthday parties. These, too, made their way around the table, and only then did he withdraw from the envelope, in a transparent plastic folder, some half dozen sample pages from his book and hand them to me.

"I work on a Macintosh," he told me. "You?"

"Still a typewriter," I said.

Though I could tell that Claire was less than captivated by Walter's personality—in the car on the way home, when I asked what she'd made of Walter, she described him as a lurid exhibitionist—she alone at the table had been following my conversation with him. My father, a ringmaster intent on talking simultaneously to everyone, was able only to tune in and out on Walter and me, and the others were no more interested in Walter than he was in them. I myself didn't know what to make of him, whether he was as forward about his Auschwitz past with everyone he met or whether what looked to Claire to be exhibitionism hadn't perhaps been galvanized a little by my father's promise of assistance from the writer son who gave his college classes books to read about the concentration camps.

"I wrote it in German," he explained as I removed the pages from the folder. "The translation I made myself. But my German by now is not that good and my English when I write is only so-so. I am giving it to my daughter to fix the English for me." Speaking softly to me alone, he said, "I don't know what my daughter will think. She does not know how I survived in Berlin. This isn't the way a child thinks of a parent. She is a married woman, of course; but, still, a father . . ."

This is what I read. *My member was enormous once again and we had only finished. . . . My fountain of juice flowed into her delicious hole. . . . Her lips descended upon my swollen prick. . . . Oh, do that to me again, she said, oh beloved, again. . . . Her dress fell, revealing to me tits more magnificent than Barbara's and bigger than Helen's. . . . I came. . . . She came. . . . It was a delirium.*

And meanwhile, I thought, there was a Holocaust going on.

"Well, Phil, what do you think?" my father asked me. At the table everyone was looking my way, though no one as earnestly as Walter.

"Haven't finished," I said.

She was starved for a man as only a woman of thirty-five can be in wartime. She bathed me in her tub. While the water drained I leaned back. As though it were a ten-course meal, she fell upon my

*penis. My son, she said, my son. I had never been
devoured like this before. Only Katrina had come
close to this. Look at it, she said, it is a wonder! I
came again. She came again. I came again.*

On and on.

When I had finished all the pages, I silently returned them to the folder. Walter said, "This is only
a sample."

"There's more."

"Much more. Could it be published?"

"You should finish before you worry about pub-
lication."

"I *am* finished. It only needs my daughter to edit
the English."

"What about Asher?" my father said to me.

I shrugged. Walter, of course, wouldn't have
dreamed of showing these pages to my father, nor
did it occur to my father to ask to read them. All he
wanted to do was to help a Jewish victim of Hitler
and a friend from the Y.

My shrug, I saw, had irritated my father—and
puzzled him, too. Was I or was I not interested in
books about the Holocaust?

"Give it to *me*, Walter," he said. "I'll take care
of it with Aaron Asher. What about David Rieff?" my
father said to me.

"Yes," I said, "there's always David."

"Do I have his phone number?" my father
asked. "Is it the old number?"

"The old number."

"So—what *do* you think?" my father asked again, no longer hiding his exasperation.

I made a gesture with my two hands that didn't mean a thing, accompanied by an agreeable smile.

"Your son is not a man to commit himself," Walter said politely to my father.

"Yeah . . ." he mumbled disgustedly and went back to his *ballaboosteh.*

On the phone just two days later, my father said, "I'm going to send you some mail. Walter was here this afternoon. He has something for you."

"Dad, no more pages, please, from the book."

"It's the coat he told you about. He left a photograph and the information. He wants me to mail it to you."

After dessert, Walter had told Claire and me that he had the perfect coat for a movie star: "Made for this year's winter collection—so special only a few women in the world could carry it off. A full-length sable, the softest, most weightless sable you've ever seen, and a wonderful shawl collar of summer ermine. I could restyle it for Miss Bloom and it would be gorgeous." It should sell, by all rights, for well over a hundred thousand, Walter told us, but he would talk to his son and they would come up with an interesting proposition. "So special, these furs," he added, "that only two such coats were ever made." "I'll take both," I told him. "I'm afraid that only one is left," Walter replied.

His humorless ardor about giving away, at rock-
bottom, this full-length summer ermine and sable
coat, the last one in the world and just what we
needed, made me think of that chapter in *Survival in
Auschwitz* in which Primo Levi describes the forbid-
den bartering and bargaining among the prisoners; a
ration of bread was the most common unit of cur-
rency, but everything from a ragged shred of a shirt
to the gold teeth in one's mouth was being continu-
ously traded in the corner of the camp farthest from
the S.S. barracks. Could not Walter, as a young
man, have been among the most brazen of those
Auschwitz traders, or was the capitalist zeal
something he'd picked up when he got to America? I said to my father, "Your friend isn't easily
discouraged."

"You know he's been to Israel forty-five times?"

"What's he selling to them?" I asked.

"You're a wise guy."

"So's Walter, if you don't mind my saying so.
This is one very mischievous Jew. Jewish mischief,
thank God, survived the camps too. Guess what his
book's about."

"I'm going to mail you the picture of the coat."

"Keep it and buy it for Lil. I said his book—
guess what it's about."

"Well, it's about his incarceration."

"No, no," I said.

"It's about his days in Germany."

"It's pornography. Did you know that?"

"I don't know anything. I didn't read any of it."

"It's all about fucking. Every page. He makes me look like a piker."

"Yeah? No kidding." He sounded, for the moment, a little stunned.

"That's why I didn't say anything when you asked me. I was sitting there having dinner with you all, and he gives me this thing, and it's pornography." I was laughing now, and my father joined in.

"And he just left about half an hour ago," my father said.

"Yeah, well, this one sucked me, this one fucked me, I had the biggest cock in Nazi Germany."

We were still laughing when my father said, "Maybe it'll be a best-seller like *Portnoy*."

"Of course. A pornographic best-seller about the Holocaust."

"Guess so."

"Well, that'll be a first," I said.

"His daughter is editing it," my father said.

"She's going to be in for a big surprise."

He was still laughing a little when he said, "I bought that cane today."

"What kind of cane?"

"Sandy wanted me to buy it. With four prongs on it."

"And have you tried it?"

"Yeah. I don't like it because you become accustomed to it. I don't want to become dependent on it."

"You used it when you took your walk? It helped?"

"Yeah, sure. It helped. I don't have to hold on to Abe. Because he's beginning to sag a little himself."

"What do you boys talk about on those walks?"

"We get talking about old times. The old comedians. The Howard Brothers. Lou Holtz. Cantor. Benny. And we sing songs together. Abe likes that. You remember Lou Holtz? He used to say, 'Vas you dere, Chollie?'"

"Is that who said that? I've often wondered. I always say it to Claire but I never knew who the comedian was. He's before my time, Lou Holtz. Vas you dere, Chollie?"

"Sure. We talk about Harry Lauder. Then I sing a song to him about Harry Lauder, and Abe joins in. That's how we walk up and down every day. Abe loved Harry Lauder. The Scotch comedian. I used to watch him when I went to the Palace in Newark. He used to come out and sing this one song. I forget it now that I have to remember. He used to come out with a bent cane and he used to sing this Scottish song. Abe loves that song. He always sings it. It was all clean fun."

"Well, there's the difference for you between old Newark and old Berlin."

"Yeah. Poor Walter."

"Don't feel too sorry for poor Walter. He can take care of himself. He's had some fun in his time."

"Yeah? You believe that stuff? You believe all those things there?"

"Don't you?"

"Who knows? Maybe he's just writing a book."

Our family plans to celebrate his birthday in Connecticut—as we'd done each August since my mother's death eight years back—had to be canceled when, as the summer wore on, his health deteriorated still further. Even with the new four-pronged cane it was now downright dangerous for him to try to move about the apartment on his own, let alone to walk outside anymore. The arm-in-arm sing-alongs with Abe abruptly came to an end and then, intermittently, he began to develop trouble when he swallowed, coughing and choking particularly hard while trying to get down liquids. He associated these difficulties with a lingering cold when, in fact, the enlarging tumor had begun to interfere with the part of the brain that controls the swallowing mechanism.

Unlike my father, I wasn't unprepared for this, since, a little more than a year before, Dr. Benjamin had warned me—after I'd said no at the hospital to the brain surgery—that the swallowing was likely to be affected next. I got in touch with Dr. Wasserman to ask what, if anything, could be done for him. Some tests were ordered and they confirmed that he had begun to aspirate what he ate and was in danger of contracting bronchial pneumonia by this taking of food or drink into his lungs through his windpipe. "It would be better," Harold Wasserman suggested to me, "if he didn't eat." When I asked—startled by his words—what that could possibly mean, Harold explained how the danger of pneumonia could be circumvented by inserting a tube into my father's stomach and feeding him that way. A gastrostomy, it was called. "And what does he do with his saliva?" I asked. "Spits it out," I was told. "It can also be cleaned out with a machine."

Now comes the pay-off, I thought, the consequences of having decided against the operation. "It's beginning to get horrible," I told my brother and for the next few weeks he and I let our father go along blaming his new problem on the cold; until the difficulty got dramatically worse—and we were assured that it would soon enough—we would not depress him further by explaining to him the real source of his trouble. He seemed himself to sense that something serious was up, however, because when I asked on the phone if eating had gotten any easier, he began to deny that it had ever become hard. "It's just that I can't drink sweet liquids," "It's just if the food is too hot," and so on. "I bring up phlegm," he said, "because of my cold. I'm not having any operation on my throat." "Nobody's proposing an operation. But you do seem to have a little swallowing problem." "I don't. I'm fine."

In the meantime, it was summer, and in the Connecticut hills I'd take a fast four-mile walk early each morning, while it was still cool, and in the late afternoon, after another day's work on a novel I had just about finished, I'd go for a thirty-minute swim in the pool. Despite my worries about my father, I hadn't felt healthier in years, and nearing the end of the revisions of *Deception*, the new novel, was the sweet relief that finishing a book always is. But early in August, when I went to take my afternoon swim one day, something unexpected happened, only this time not to my father but to me—after just one easy lap, my head was splitting, my heart was pounding madly, and I could barely catch my breath. Clinging to the edge of the pool, I told myself, "It's anxiety. What are you so anxious about?"—the sort of question that people in physical trouble had the sense not to bother about before the advent of the psychoso-mologists. What lay in store for my father had debi-litated more than just my morale: I felt dreadful, I told myself, because his months and months of mis-ery with the brain tumor were to culminate now in having a feeding tube inserted permanently into his stomach.

My diagnosis was wrong. I felt dreadful after only one lap because over the course of fifty-six years virtually every major artery to my heart had become eighty to a hundred percent occluded and I was not far from a huge heart attack. Twenty-four hours after I climbed out of the swimming pool, gasping for air, I was saved from the heart attack—and from preced-ing my father to the grave—and he was spared having to bury me—by an emergency quintuple bypass operation.

At 2:00 A.M. on the night before the surgery, when the symptoms took an alarming turn and some half-dozen interns, residents, and nurses began circling busily around the instruments monitoring my worsening condition, a call went out to the surgeon to see if he wanted to change his plans and operate immediately. I realized that never had I been more at one with my father than I was at that moment: not since college, when I used to smuggle him secretly into class with me, the intellectual homunculus for whose development I felt as responsible as I did for my own, had our lives been, if not identical, so intermeshed and spookily interchangeable. Helpless at the center of this little medical hubbub, I confronted, with a clarifying shock, the inevitability in which, for him, every second of existence was awash now.

The difference, of course, was that *after* the surgery I felt reborn—at once reborn and as though I had given birth. My heart, which for any number of years prior to the operation, had apparently been performing on as little as twenty percent of its normal blood supply, was being permeated by all the blood it could want. I would smile to myself in the hospital bed at night, envisioning my heart as a tiny infant suckling itself on this blood coursing unobstructed now through the newly attached arteries borrowed from my leg. This, I thought, is what the thrill must be like nursing one's own infant—the strident, drumlike, postoperative heartbeat was not mine but *its*. So that the night nurse couldn't hear, I whispered to that baby, just under my breath, "Suck, yes, suck, suck away, it's yours, all yours, for you . . ." and never in my life had I been happier.

I don't know how much of that recurrent fantasy and its accompanying litany was a consequence of the euphoria of having had my life saved and how much was the lingering aftereffect of five hours under heavy anesthesia, but during those first few nights, when the pain in my chest wall made continuous sleep impossible, the thought that I was giving suck to my own newborn heart provided hours of the most intense pleasure, sessions during which I did not have to use any imagination at all to feel myself androgynously partaking of the most delirious maternal joy. It strikes me now, looking back, that in the exuberant reveries of those first postoperative nights, I was as near to being the double of my own nurturing mother as, during the anxious, uncertain hours on the eve of the bypass, I had come to feeling myself *transposed*, interchangeable with—even a sacrificial proxy for—my failing father, choking on his mortality at the dinner table. I was never a heart patient alone in that bed: I was a family of four.

I had hoped to keep the news from my father until I was entirely recovered—or for good, if that seemed warranted—but it was impossible. On the Thursday evening before the operation—just a few hours before I took the bad turn—I had phoned him from my bed in the coronary care unit and, pretending that I was home in Connecticut, told him that I had been asked, at the last minute, to fill in at a literary conference for a writer who'd become ill and that I'd be away in New Haven all weekend, probably unable to get to a phone until I was back on Sunday evening. "How much they paying you?" he asked. "Ten thousand bucks," I said, picking a somewhat inflated figure out of the air, one that was bound to please him and—I thought rightly—to distract him from asking anything further. "Good," he said, but with the implication that it was no more than I deserved. Just some sixty or so hours after the operation, on Sunday evening, I phoned again, explaining that if my voice was weak, it was from having talked all weekend at the conference. "They pay you?" "You bet. In singles. Gave it to me in a wheelbarrow." "Well," he replied, laughing, "that was a profitable weekend."

For the next few days, I continued to convince him on the phone each morning that I was leading my regular life—until, that is, the hospital public affairs office rang my room one afternoon to tell me that they had just had calls from the *News* and the *Post* asking for details about me. Though the public affairs officer assured me that she had given them no information, she wanted to let me know that there was likely to be something in the papers anyway. For fear of what might happen if my father, frail and vulnerable as he now was, came unsuspecting upon the news in a gossip column the next day—or got it from someone telephoning to talk to him about what they'd just read about me in the paper—I summoned up all my strength and telephoned New Jersey.

When I told him that I had had a successful coronary bypass operation (I skipped the quintuple part for the time being), he couldn't get his bearings momentarily.

"But who have I been talking to?"

I explained that it had been me, myself, phoning him, just as I was doing now, from my hospital bed. I assured him that I was coming along excellently and told him that the surgeon expected me to be home by the end of a week.

To my surprise then, he got angry. "Remember when you were in college and Mother had the operation and we didn't tell you? Remember what you said when you found out?"

"I don't, no."

"You said, 'Are we a family or aren't we a family?' You got on your high horse. You said, 'Don't ever try to "spare" me again.' You gave us a real tongue-lashing."

"Look, you're none the worse for not having had to sweat it out while I was in the operating room."

"How long were you in the operating room?"

Lopping off a couple of hours, I told him. "And you didn't need that wait," I said. "You've got enough to deal with right now."

"That's not for you to decide."

"Herm, I decided it," I said with a laugh, trying to lighten things up.

But he remained serious—even ominous. "Well, don't do it again," he warned me, as though all of life still lay before us.

Each day and each night while I was in the hospital, and during the first few weeks when I was slowly convalescing at home, I prayed directly to him. "Don't die. Don't die until I get my strength back. Don't die until I can do it right. Don't die while I'm helpless." Sometimes on the phone from the hospital I had to restrain myself from saying it to him out loud. I believe now that he understood what it was I was silently asking of him.

"How are *you* feeling?" I'd ask him. "Me?" he replied—"I'm great. I gave Abe a ninety-fourth birthday party. Ingrid made a pork roll and parsleyed potatoes. Seth and Ruth came, Rita, Abe, Ingrid, me, and Lil. We had a good time. Abe can eat, God bless him. He can walk and he can eat and the next day he even remembered the party."

Some six weeks later, when I was able to travel over to see him, he surprised me again, though this time by being almost childishly apologetic. I couldn't figure out what had him so chagrined, partly because I myself was so dismayed at the changes that had taken place in him since only the last time I'd been there. I would say it was as though a year had passed if I couldn't just as easily have said, looking at him, that it was a lifetime. He who had given Abe a ninety-

fourth birthday party had himself become one of the
aged whose age is incalculable, little more than a
shrunken thing with a crushed face, wearing a black
eye patch and sitting completely inert, almost unrec-
ognizable now, even to me. From the way he was
propped up in his usual spot at the end of the sofa, it
seemed unlikely that he could get himself moving
from there without being lifted onto his feet. A toe that
had been painfully broken the month before—he'd
blacked out in the bathroom and fallen again—was
only just beginning to heal. I saw later that even with
the aid of his brand-new walker, he could barely loco-
mote himself, by himself, further than a foot or two.

On the bureau across from the sofa was the en-
largement of the fifty-two-year-old snapshot, taken
with a box camera at the Jersey shore, that my
brother and I also had framed and situated promi-
nently in our houses. We are posing in our bathing
suits, one Roth directly behind the other, in the yard
outside the Bradley Beach rooming house where our
family rented a bedroom and kitchen privileges for a
month each summer. This is August of 1937. We are
four, nine, and thirty-six. The three of us rise upward
to form a V, my two tiny sandals its pointed base,
and the width of my father's solid shoulders—between which Sandy's pixyish bright face is exactly
centered—the letter's two impressive serifs. Yes, V
for Victory is written all over that picture: for Victory, for Vacation, for upright, unbent Verticality!
There we are, the male line, unimpaired and happy,
ascending from nascency to maturity!

To unite into a single image the robust solidity of the man in the picture with that strickenness on the sofa was and was not an impossibility. Trying with all my mental strength to join the two fathers and make them one was a bewildering, even hellish job. And yet I suddenly did feel (or made myself feel) that I could perfectly well remember (or make myself think I remembered) the very moment when that picture had been taken, over half a century before. I could even believe (or make myself believe) that our lives only seemed to have filtered through time, that everything was actually happening simultaneously, that I was as much back in Bradley with him towering over me as here in Elizabeth with him all but broken at my feet.

"What is it?" I asked when I realized that, merely from seeing me, he was upset enough to cry. "Dad—I'm fine now," I said. "You can tell that. Look at me. *Look*. Dad, what's the matter?"

"I should have been there," he told me in a breaking voice, the words barely words now because of what the paralysis had made of his mouth. "I should have been there!" he repeated, this time with fury.

He meant by my side at the hospital.

He died three weeks later. During a twelve-hour ordeal that began just before midnight on October 24, 1989, and ended just after noon the next day, he fought for every breath with an awesome eruption, a final display, of his lifelong obstinate tenacity. It was something to see.

Early on the morning of his death, when I arrived at the hospital emergency room to which he had been rushed from his bedroom at home, I was confronted by an attending physician prepared to take "extraordinary measures" and to put him on a breathing machine. Without it there was no hope, though, needless to say—the doctor added—the machine wasn't going to reverse the progress of the tumor, which appeared to have begun to attack his respiratory function. The doctor also informed me that, by law, once my father had been hooked up to the machine he would not be disconnected, unless he could once again sustain breathing on his own. A decision had to be made immediately and, since my brother was still en route by plane from Chicago, by me alone.

And I, who had explained to my father the provisions of the living will and got him to sign it, didn't know what to do. How could I say no to the machine if it meant that he needn't continue to endure this agonizing battle to breathe? How could I take it on myself to decide that my father should be finished with life, life which is ours to know just once? Far from invoking the living will, I was nearly on the verge of ignoring it and saying, "Anything! Anything!"

I asked the doctor to leave me alone with my father, or as alone as he and I could be in the middle of the emergency room bustle. As I sat there and watched him struggle to go on living, I tried to focus on what the tumor had done with him already. This wasn't difficult, given that he looked on that stretcher as though by then he'd been through a hundred rounds with Joe Louis. I thought about the misery that was sure to come, provided he could even be kept alive on a respirator. I saw it all, all, and yet I had to sit there for a very long time before I leaned as close to him as I could get and, with my lips to his sunken, ruined face, found it in me finally to whisper, "Dad, I'm going to have to let you go." He'd been unconscious for several hours and couldn't hear me, but, shocked, amazed, and weeping, I repeated it to him again and then again, until I believed it myself.

After that, all I could do was to follow his stretcher up to the room where they put him and sit by the bedside. Dying is work and he was a worker. Dying is horrible and my father was dying. I held his hand, which at least still felt like his hand; I stroked his forehead, which at least still looked like his forehead; and I said to him all sorts of things that he could no longer register. Luckily, there wasn't anything I told him that morning that he didn't already know.

Later in the day, at the bottom of a bureau drawer in my father's bedroom, my brother came upon a shallow box containing two neatly folded prayer shawls. These he hadn't parted with. These

he hadn't ferreted off to the Y locker room or given
away to one of his great-nephews. The older tallis I
took home with me and we buried him in the other.
When the mortician, at the house, asked us to pick
out a suit for him, I said to my brother, "A suit? He's
not going to the office. No, no suit—it's senseless."
He should be buried in a shroud, I said, thinking that
was how his parents had been buried and how Jews
were buried traditionally. But as I said it I wondered
if a shroud was any less senseless—he wasn't Orthodox and his sons weren't religious at all—and if it
wasn't perhaps pretentiously literary and a little hys-
terically sanctimonious as well. I thought how bi-
zarrely out-of-character an urban earthling like my
insurance-man father, a sturdy man rooted all his life
in everydayness, would look in a shroud even while I
understood that that was the idea. But as nobody
opposed me and as I hadn't the audacity to say,
"Bury him naked," we used the shroud of our ances-
tors to clothe his corpse.

I dreamed I was standing on a pier in a shadowy
group of unescorted children who may or may not
have been waiting to be evacuated. The pier was
down in Port Newark, but the Port Newark of some
fifty years ago, where I had been taken by my father
and my Uncle Ed to see the ships anchored in the
bay that opened in the distance to the Statue of Liberty and the Atlantic. It was always a surprise to me,

as a small child, to be reminded that Newark was a coastal city, since the port was beyond the swamplands, on the far side of the new Newark airstrip and remote from life in the neighborhoods. To be taken down to the harbor and on to the wharves to look up at the ships and out beyond to the bay was to be put in touch momentarily with a geographical vastness that you couldn't imagine while playing stoop ball with your little pals on our cozy, clannish street of two-and-a-half-family houses.

In the dream, a boat, a medium-size, heavily armored, battle-gray boat, some sort of old American warship stripped of its armaments and wholly disabled, floated imperceptibly toward the shore. I was expecting my father to be on the ship, somehow to be among the crew, but there was no life on board and no sign anywhere of anyone in command. The dead-silent picture, a portrait of the aftermath of a disaster, was frightening and eerie: a ghostly hulk of a ship, cleared by some catastrophe of all living things, aiming toward the shore with only the current to guide it, and we on the pier who may or may not have been children gathered together to be evacuated. The mood was heartbreaking in exactly the way it had been when I was twelve and, only weeks before the triumph of V-E Day, President Roosevelt died of a cerebral hemorrhage. Draped in black bunting, the train moving F.D.R.'s casket up from Washington to Hyde Park had passed with lumbering solemnity through the bereaved crowd squeezed in

beside the tracks downtown—during those silent
seconds on its journey north, consecrating even
workaday Newark. Ultimately the dream became unbearable and I woke up, despondent and frightened
and sad—whereupon I understood that it wasn't that
my father was aboard the ship but that my father
was the ship. And to be evacuated was physio-
logically just that: to be expelled, to be ejected, to be
born.

I lay awake until dawn. The dream had disturbed my sleep only hours before the morning at the
end of July when my father was to have the second
MRI of his brain. Dr. Benjamin had ordered the pictures after I had asked Harold Wasserman to consult
Benjamin about my father's swallowing problem.
I phoned him after he got home from the MRI and
when I asked, "How did it go?" he replied, "Old
people, young people, healthy-looking people, sick-
looking people—and everybody there has something
inside them."

To have dreamed of my father's death on the
eve of that second MRI wasn't at all remarkable, nor,
really, was the incarnation that the dream had
worked upon his body. I lay in bed till it was light,
thinking of all the family history compressed into that
snippet of silent dream-film: just about every major
theme of his life was encapsulated there, everything
of significance to both of us, starting with his immigrant parents' transatlantic crossing in steerage, ex-
tending to his grueling campaign to get ahead, the

battle to make good against so many obstructive forces—as a poor boy robbed of serious schooling, as a Jewish working man in the Gentile insurance colossus—and ending with his transformation, by the brain tumor, into an enfeebled wreck.

The defunct warship drifting blindly into shore . . . this is not a picture of my father, at the end of his life, that my wide-awake mind, with its resistance to plaintive metaphor and poeticized analogy, was ever likely to have licensed. Rather, it was sleep that, in its wisdom, kindly delivered up to me this childishly simple vision so rich with truth and crystallized my own pain so aptly in the figure of a small, fatherless evacuee on the Newark docks, as stunned and bereft as the entire nation had once been at the passing of a heroic president.

Then, one night some six weeks later, at around 4:00 A.M., he came in a hooded white shroud to reproach me. He said, "I should have been dressed in a suit. You did the wrong thing." I awakened screaming. All that peered out from the shroud was the displeasure in his dead face. And his only words were a rebuke: I had dressed him for eternity in the wrong clothes.

In the morning I realized that he had been alluding to this book, which, in keeping with the unseemliness of my profession, I had been writing all the while he was ill and dying. The dream was telling me that, if not in my books or in my life, at least in my dreams I would live perennially as his little son, with

the conscience of a little son, just as he would remain
alive there not only as my father but as *the* father,
sitting in judgment on whatever I do.

You must not forget anything.